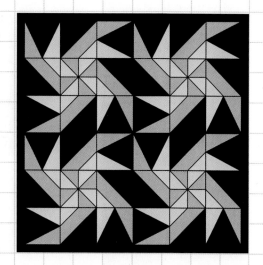

PATTERN PLAY

Creating Your Own Quilts

By Doreen Speckmann

C&T PUBLISHING

Copyright © 1993 Doreen Speckmann

Edited by Harold Nadel

Technical information researched by Joyce Lytle and Barbara Kuhn

Photography by Sharon Risedorph, San Francisco

Book design by Rose Sheifer Graphic Productions,
    Walnut Creek, California

Computer graphics by Peter Speckmann and by Edge Design,
    Cupertino, California

Cover design by Meridian, Orinda, California

ISBN 0-914881-70-1

Library of Congress Cataloging-in-Publication Data

Speckmann, Doreen.
    Pattern play / by Doreen Speckmann.
        p. cm.
    ISBN 0-914881-70-1
    1. Quilting—Patterns—Design. 2. Patchwork—Patterns—Design.
3. Quilting—Patterns. 4. Patchwork—Patterns.   I. Title.
TT835. S643 1993
756.9 ' 7041—dc20   93-5633
                                                        CIP

Aldus SuperPaint is a registered trademark of Aldus Corporation.
Macintosh SE is a registered trademark of Apple Computer, Inc.
Pfaff Creative 1475 CD is a registered trademark of Pfaff Corp.
Schmetz is a name brand of Ferd. Schmetz GmbH., Germany.
Singer Featherweight is a registered trademark of the
    Singer Sewing Company.
Spray-Mount is a registered trademark of the 3M Company.
Star Thread is a registered trademark of Coats American Inc.

Published by C & T Publishing
P. O. Box 1456
Lafayette, California 94549

Printed in Hong Kong

10 9 8 7 6 5 4 3 2 1

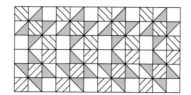

Table of Contents

INTRODUCTION

My main intention in this book is to tell you why I started to design my own quilts, and how I went about doing so. I also want to show you how I make the transition from paper scribblings to fabric and the finished quilt. I think my method is easy to understand and an eye-opener to those who have felt limited by the strict traditions of quiltmaking. It is my firm belief that the true traditions of quiltmaking demand that we take what was given us, make changes and additions, and pass our new knowledge on to the next generation of quilters.

First, a little of my quiltmaking history. In 1976 I had no intention of becoming a quiltmaker. My preconceptions of quilting were built upon myth and misinformation:

1. Only Little Old Ladies on metal folding chairs in church basements made quilts. (I was 26 at the time, and 40 still looked like over-the-hill to me.)
2. "It isn't a quilt unless every stitch is made by hand." I had cut my teeth by sewing Barbie doll clothes, made all of my own clothes, and felt completely at ease at the sewing machine. And I already had enough handwork (knitting, crocheting, needlepoint, counted thread) to last a lifetime.
3. It was already too late for me to start. I had heard rumors of quilts that were started by one generation and finished by another.
4. If, by stitching diligence, I was able to complete a top, I would have to permanently install a nine-foot-square quilt frame in the middle of my living room.

This all proves that a little knowledge is dangerous, and that I was a pretty silly person. What no one could have told me then was that I had all the pre-quiltmaking conditions: I already bought fabric I had no use for, and I have an unnatural attraction to office supplies.

So, in January 1977, while expecting my first baby, I began my first quilt. It was my intention to be the Perfect Mother. I thought the Perfect Baby should have a quilt that it would treasure for a lifetime—and that it would be easier to repair a patchwork quilt than re-knit a thermal blanket. I chose a pattern that was easy to sew on the sewing machine (Patience Corner), basted in two layers of batting over a 1" gingham backing, and quilted in ¼" stitches. The result was far from a thing of beauty, but I was hooked on quiltmaking.

I read all the books and magazines I could get my hands on so I could learn to "do it right." When they told me to make templates out of sandpaper, I made templates out of sandpaper. When instructed to store all my templates in envelopes, I bought wonderful manila ones with the little pincers on the back and found the perfect box so I could run my fingers through my patterns at will. It didn't take me long to figure out that I had a boxful of dozens of the same templates.

The light dawned on me that, if the templates were interchangeable, so were the design units. Shoofly became Churn Dash when I replaced the middle squares with rectangles and Prairie Queen when a four-patch was inserted. Of course, there were blocks that didn't fit into my marvelous "new" system, such as the hexagon family and eight-pointed stars. I realized that there were different families of quilt blocks that all operated under their own rules. Along came Jinny Beyer's *Patchwork Patterns*, which clarified things even further. Though I was a little disappointed that I had re-invented the wheel, the world of quilt design was no longer a mystery.

The added benefit of working all this out was that I had a firmer grasp on the construction process. No longer at the mercy of templates from books and magazines, I was able to create my own templates and designs as well as develop an efficient and accurate piecing strategy. I also enjoy the little control I now have over the quiltmaking process. There is so much I don't have any control over (oil prices, who is elected president, the homeless, what we do with our nuclear waste) that the prospect of making my own designs and turning those designs into quilts is exciting and fulfilling.

In this book, I will introduce you to an easy and fun way to design your own blocks on graph paper, then put those blocks into interesting quilt designs. I will discuss fabric selection and the techniques necessary for turning your graph paper quilts into real ones. As an additional bonus, you will find scale drawings and photos of some of my favorite quilts, complete with yardages and size-change options. Most important, I want you to enjoy the design process as much as I do, to see for yourself how one idea leads to another and another, and to make unique quilts that you will be proud of.

UNDERSTANDING BLOCK DESIGN

The first stage in designing new quilt blocks is to look to the traditions of quiltmaking for inspiration. When I started quilting, I couldn't make heads or tails of block design. Each block had a name, and each seemed independent of all others. Fortunately, it didn't take me long to see that patterns fall into families. The hexagon family (based on equilateral triangles) operates by a specific set of rules, as do all the variations of the eight-pointed stars and circular wedge designs (Dresden Plate to Mariner's Compass).

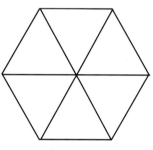

hexagon

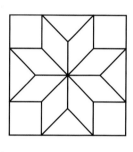

8-pointed star

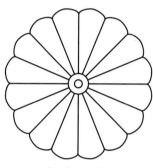

circular wedge

The family of design that I am most attracted to is grid-based. The elements are easy to see, easy to manipulate and draw on graph paper and, best of all, easy to piece. Grid-based blocks include nine-patch, four-patch, five-patch, and so on. We can identify them because they can be divided into equal squares. Quilt books are already full of variations of patch design blocks.

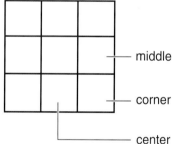

middle

corner

center

Certain facts became clear as I studied traditional patch design blocks. First, nine-patch blocks are created by repeating units or components, arranged by placing one unit in the corners, another in the middles, and another in the center. Every time a change is made, there is a new name for the block. Shoofly becomes Churn Dash and then Prairie Queen with a simple change of components.

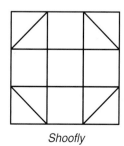

Shoofly

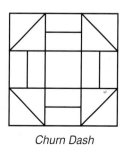

Churn Dash

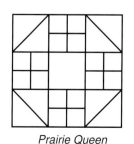

Prairie Queen

By changing the position of the big triangles from the corners to the middles, the block is renamed Contrary Wife. With the addition of four-patches to the corners and center, it becomes Jacob's Ladder. When the four-patches are replaced with *Ice Cream Cones*, the block could be called X-Wing Fighter, and I have created a block that wasn't in any book I owned. Could it be that all of the quilt blocks haven't yet been invented?

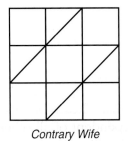
Contrary Wife

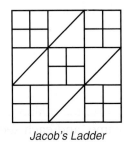
Jacob's Ladder

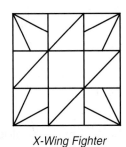
X-Wing Fighter

DESIGNING ON GRAPH PAPER

When we know how to do this with ease, half the problem of designing original blocks and quilts is conquered.

Use ¼" graph paper. Set up the grid 3 x 3, 4 x 4, or 5 x 5 by making each unit in the grid cover four graph-paper squares. This size is perfect, because the units are small enough for you to draw straight lines without using a ruler. The blocks are small enough to fit many on a page, but large enough to add detail and see the effect of patterning. (Also, blocks that are drawn too large take forever to color in.)

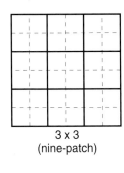
3 x 3
(nine-patch)

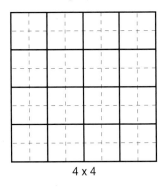
4 x 4

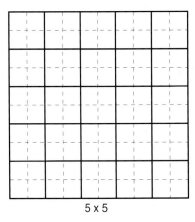
5 x 5

Practice drawing a few traditional nine-patches to get the feel. First, set up the grid. Look for the repeating units and their orientation to the center of the block. Using a fine-point marker, draw your lines without a ruler: use the intersections of the graph paper as a guide. (Using a ruler slows you down and keeps you from seeing what you are doing.) Draw the middles, then the corners, and finally the center square.

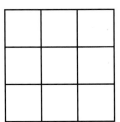 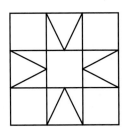 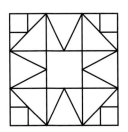 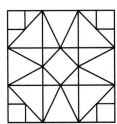

If you would rather manipulate pieces of paper instead of drawing on graph paper, you can make a set of block components. Make copies of the components on pages 157-159, glue them to a piece of poster board, then cut up the squares. You can set up blocks the same way you would on graph paper. It helps if you spray a blank sheet of paper with Spray-Mount®, making a tacky surface for arranging the small squares. Use ice-cube trays to sort out the pieces by shapes. Now, instead of drawing in corners, middles, and centers, you can pick up the pieces and place them.

This is a great way to work if you hate to draw and are working on a table. You will have to transfer the block to graph paper eventually, in order to copy it and work it into a quilt design. It just isn't practical to construct a whole multi-block quilt design from cut-and-glued squares. The advantage to working this way for many is spontaneity. Your fingers may pick up the right pieces when your brain is stalled.

Computer Options

Any attempt to give specific directions for designing on the computer is doomed to obsolescence. But anyone who has ever worked with even the simplest computer graphics program knows these blocks and units are perfect for computer designing. The most basic paint/draw program would meet your needs. What you want it to do is "snap a grid"—computer lingo for creating graph paper with points instead of lines; you need a straight-line drawing tool that will leave a line between two points of graph paper. When you have drawn the block, you should be able to pick it up and repeat it (as if you had a rubber stamp). And, lastly, you should be able to print it. Of course, there are more bells and whistles available—scanners, color printers that could enhance the computer design process, and more tricks and gadgets are being developed as you read this. I use a Macintosh SE® computer and Aldus SuperPaint® 3.0. We have added more memory (to accommodate graphics) and a full-page monitor so I can see the whole design. Check out the new quilt-specific programs as well.

CREATING ORIGINAL BLOCKS FROM TRADITIONAL COMPONENTS

Let's look at the basic components that are a part of our quiltmaking heritage and the basis of all the quilts I design. Most are familiar shapes found in traditional quilt blocks; a few are adaptations of the traditional ones. You'll notice that the names for some are purely descriptive, while others make no sense at all. Years ago, if I had known I would eventually write this book, I might have just given them numbers (it would have been so much easier). But I started giving some of these components goofy names—*Peaky & Spike, Wingy Things, Mutt & Jeff*—to make them easier for me to remember. (It's a family problem: none of my five brothers and sisters were ever called by their given names.) I'll introduce you to each of the components and give a little background description for the name. You can re-name them to suit your tastes and memory.

There is nothing free-form about them. All of the lines that create the shapes within the components either start in a corner and end in a corner, start in a middle and end in a middle, or start in a corner and end in a middle. Practice drawing the components on graph paper now, while you become familiar with the names. They are pictured on the front inside cover flap.

- *Square*—An easy one: no lines to draw, no pieces to sew!
- *Rectangles*
- *Four-Patch*
- *Half-Square Triangle*
- *Eight Half-Square Triangles*—This is a *Four-Patch* divided into *Half-Square Triangles*.
- *Wingy Things*—This is a *Four-Patch* with opposite squares divided into triangles, named because it struck me as insect-like.
- *Night & Noon*—This is a little confusing, because there is also a block by this name; when you take the Ohio Star out of the traditional Night & Noon block, you are left with these stripy things in the corners.
- *Half Night & Noon*—Half of the previous component, pieced with a *Half-Square Triangle*.
- *Little House*—Because it looks like one.
- *Center Diamond*—Actually a square on point; it reminded me of the Amish Center Diamond quilt.
- *Trickies* (or *Quarter-Square Triangles*)—These are right triangles with templates based on the length of the long side instead of the shorter sides.
- *Card Trick* (*Half-Square* plus two *Quarter-Squares*)—Another confusing name, because there is a block also named Card Trick. The component is in the middle of the Card Trick block.
- *Flying Geese*—When rows of these are linked, the traditional design is also called Flying Geese.
- *Chevron*
- *Peaky & Spike*—These are my favorites: the skinny triangles are *Peakies* and the large isosceles triangle is *Spike*. (Friends in Denver pointed out to this poor flatlander that *Spike* looks more like a mountain peak, and *Peakies* really resemble railroad spikes. What they said clearly makes sense. Then I realized that I had a very clear picture in my mind of who (not what) *Peaky* and *Spike* really are. So, they stay as baptized.

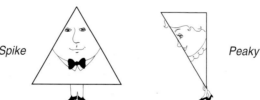

- *Ice Cream Cone I*—This cone is empty; note the small triangle in the corner.
- *Ice Cream Cone II*—The cone is full.
- *Mutt & Jeff (Left* and *Right)*—Named for the comic characters, and derived from *Ice Cream Cone I*.
- *Sliver (Left* and *Right*)—So named because it is a really skinny piece, actually half of *Ice Cream Cone II*.
- *Storm Corner*—This is the corner unit of the traditional Storm at Sea block.
- *Birds*—Derived from the traditional quilt design called Birds in Air.
- *Ribbon, Corner Gone, One Peaky Left* or *Right*—These are good linking pieces.

Feel free to invent your own additional components. You'll probably notice that there are no curved-seam components (because I can't stand sewing curved seams). But curved seams could turn this concept on its ear. The possibilities are endless. Take a few minutes <u>now</u> to draw each of these units on graph paper.

Now we're ready to start designing original blocks. Draw at least twelve empty nine-patches (refer back to the section Designing on Graph Paper, on page 7, for specific directions). Look through the components for one that is comfortable or grabs your eye. Draw it into the middle position of all of your nine-patches.

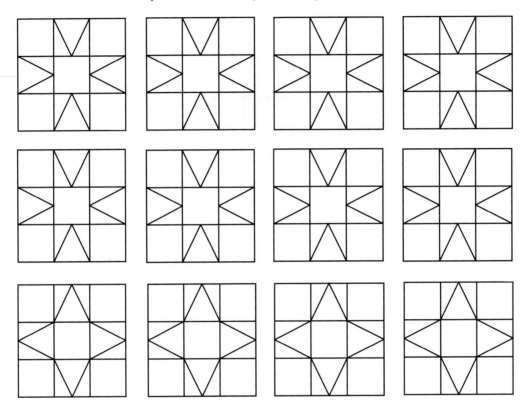

If it is a component that has a direction, such as *Peaky & Spike*, *Flying Geese*, or *Chevron*, flip its direction in a few of the squares.

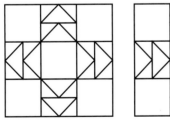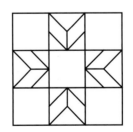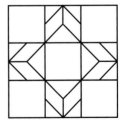

Flying Geese　　　　　　　　　　*Chevron*

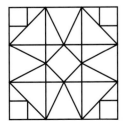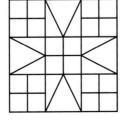

Storm at Sea　　*54-40 or Fight*

Now look to the other block components to fill up the empty squares. (You may not feel inspired to greatness right away.) At first I tried so hard not to replicate a block I already knew from traditional design that I just sat staring at the paper. I've since learned that it is easier to draw them and get them out of my system. Then I am free to experiment with other shapes.

Draw in the corner units first; then look for an appropriate center unit. Turn these shapes, too, if possible. *Ice Cream Cones II* can point in toward the center, or out.

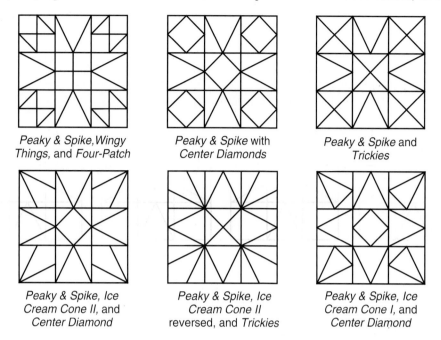

Peaky & Spike, Wingy Things, and *Four-Patch*

Peaky & Spike with *Center Diamonds*

Peaky & Spike and *Trickies*

Peaky & Spike, Ice Cream Cone II, and *Center Diamond*

Peaky & Spike, Ice Cream Cone II reversed, and *Trickies*

Peaky & Spike, Ice Cream Cone I, and *Center Diamond*

You may want to put a spin on the corner units. (This is easier to show than to explain.)

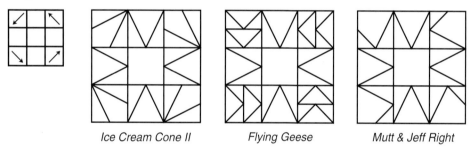

Ice Cream Cone II

Flying Geese

Mutt & Jeff Right

I work at design with as much concentration as I would give a crossword puzzle (if I could do crossword puzzles). The trick is to let one idea lead to another and then another. Instead of wondering what it would look like to put *Night & Noons* with *Peaky & Spike,* just do it. Then play with the directions and positions within the nine-patch.

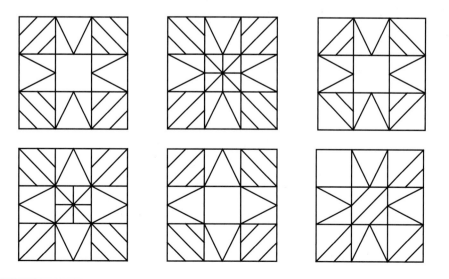

When I thought I had done everything I could possibly do with *Peaky & Spike* and *Night & Noon*, I wondered what would happen if I really mixed things up, putting *Peaky & Spikes* in the corners and *Night & Noons* in the middles. The result was one of my favorite blocks, the basis for the quilt "Barbed Wire" (page 123).

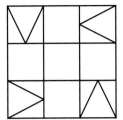 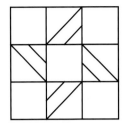 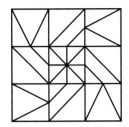

Doing the unexpected is at the core of creativity. If you think a piece should go a certain way, do just the opposite. Sometimes this works out, and the new block is dynamite; at other times, it may be merely ho-hum. I don't worry about the duds: it's only a few lines on a piece of paper. At this point, you shouldn't be worried about color, fabric, or yardage. Save all these ideas (even the duds); you may revive them in another quilt block. And you may, as I did, come back to an idea.

A few years after making the "Barbed Wire" quilt, I was playing on graph paper. I remembered how well it had gone when I put *Peaky & Spikes* and *Night & Noons* in what I had thought were the wrong places. This time I put *Ice Cream Cones I* in the middles instead of the corners—where I thought they belonged. At first, I thought the drawing was a dud, because my eyes had gotten used to seeing the *Ice Cream Cone* shape surrounded by background. I put it away and, when I later came back to it, I saw the short-legged long-legged star instead.

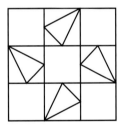 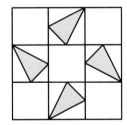

By eliminating one line from the *Ice Cream Cone* the effect was heightened and, in the process, I created a new block component: *Mutt & Jeff*. With a *Center Diamond* unit in the center, I had a new star design—an unusual lopsided one. This block was used in the quilt "Sea of Stars" (page 127).

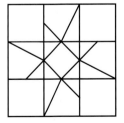

Sometime later, I went back to the *Ice Cream Cones* in the middles of the nine-patch. This time, instead of taking away a line, I added one to the corner units. The new line from the tip of the short point to the tip of the next long point actually created the original

Peaky shape. The appearance, though, was the same lopsided eight-pointed star, now squished into a block slightly on point. You can probably see it more clearly with shading.

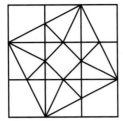 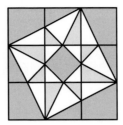

With a little experimenting, I discovered that, by turning the *Ice Cream Cones* in the opposite direction, I could spin the star to the right as well as the left. You can see both of these blocks put to use in "Topsy-Turvy" (page 122) and "Peaky & Spike Go to the Great Barrier Reef" (page 124).

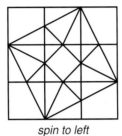 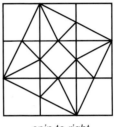

spin to left   *spin to right*

For the star, we always need the right-handed *Mutt & Jeff*, never the left-handed. Since I am used to working with *Mutt & Jeff* as a reversible unit, I was distressed in cutting out the pieces. The best new block I could imagine was one that used both right- and left-handed *Mutt & Jeffs*.

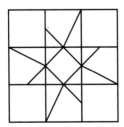

I put reversed units in two of the middles of the nine-patch. Then I added *Ice Cream Cones II* to the corners and center. The middles not filled with *Mutt & Jeff* have *Ice Cream Cones II* split down the center. The block shows off best when set on point (page 124). Later in the book you'll see further adaptations of what looks to me like a lily.

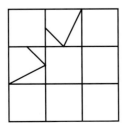 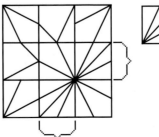

I've chosen to show you all this not only to help explain the quilts that follow but, more importantly, to show the progression of an idea. I would never have drawn the lily if I hadn't taken *Peaky & Spike* and *Night & Noon* through their paces. Then "Barbed Wire" broke the rules and looked good. From "Barbed Wire" to the Mutt & Jeff Star, and then my laziness in cutting led to the lily. Your own ideas can follow similar paths once you take the first step. Don't ever discount an idea because you're sure it will look dumb. You may be on the threshold to a whole new bunch of quilts that you never imagined. Take your graph paper along with you and doodle anytime you have a few minutes. I can't impress on you strongly enough that the only real way to learn something is to do it and do it and do it. I have forgotten the pages I've filled with blocks that will never be committed to fabric. I am not normally very assertive, but I insist that you start this <u>now</u>.

A Quick Review

1. Look over block components.
2. Draw twelve empty nine-patches.
3. Pick one of the components.
4. Draw into the middles.
5. Turn the component if possible in some blocks.
6. Look for other components to fill corners.
7. Do the unexpected; don't be disappointed, and don't give up.

Here are some examples, but certainly not the limits, of what can happen when you progress from traditional blocks to their offspring.

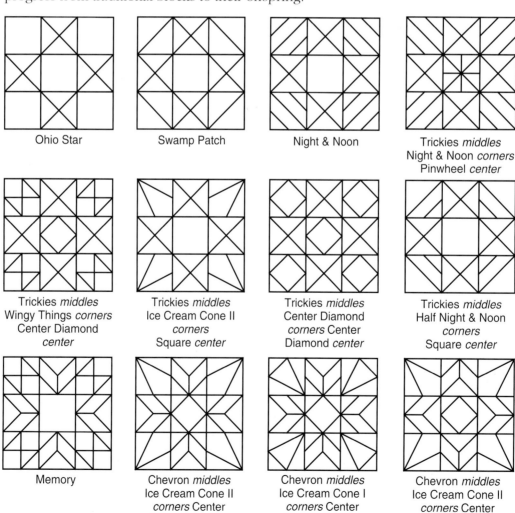

Ohio Star

Swamp Patch

Night & Noon

Trickies *middles*
Night & Noon *corners*
Pinwheel *center*

Trickies *middles*
Wingy Things *corners*
Center Diamond
center

Trickies *middles*
Ice Cream Cone II
corners
Square *center*

Trickies *middles*
Center Diamond
corners Center
Diamond *center*

Trickies *middles*
Half Night & Noon
corners
Square *center*

Memory

Chevron *middles*
Ice Cream Cone II
corners Center
Diamond *center*

Chevron *middles*
Ice Cream Cone I
corners Center
Diamond *center*

Chevron *middles*
Ice Cream Cone II
corners Center
Diamond *center*

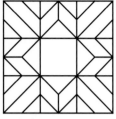

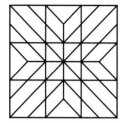

Chevron *middles*
Night & Noon *corners*
Square *center*

Chevron *middles*
Half Night & Noon
corners
Center Diamond *center*

Chevron *middles*
Night & Noon *corners*
Pinwheel *center*

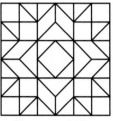
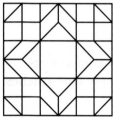
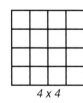
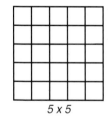

Chevron *middles*
Wingy Things *corners*
Center Diamond
center

Chevron *middles*
Half Wingy Things
corners
Square *center*

EXPANSION

So far we have been working exclusively with nine-patch blocks. A lot can be done with the nine-patch, but a new world opens up when we move to larger grids. There's more space for more components, and thus a more visually complicated block. When you think you've done everything you could possibly do with the 3 x 3 grid block, you'll love the expanded grid.

There are three ways to expand blocks. They are all good ways to work, but I have to put them in some kind of order. Read through, pick one, and try it.

Method I: The first step is to draw 3 x 3, 4 x 4, and 5 x 5 blocks. It would be a good idea to draw at least four sets of these grids so you won't quit playing too soon.

3 x 3

4 x 4

5 x 5

Now choose a traditional nine-patch block and analyze it for basic components. I'll use the Card Trick block designed by Jeffrey Gutcheon. You will also find it called Air Castle when the center is changed from *Trickies* to *Center Diamond*.

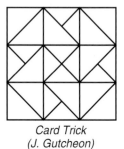
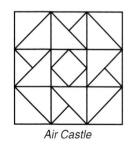

Card Trick
(J. Gutcheon)

Air Castle

Analyze the block for components. Card Trick is composed of *Half-Square Tri-angles* in the corner spots, *Card Trick* in the middles, and *Trickies* in the center.

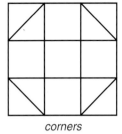

corners

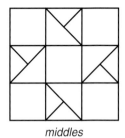

middles

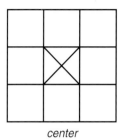

center

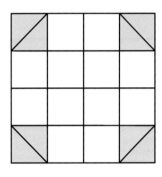

When you understand that much, you can put these same units into a larger grid block. First draw *Half-Square Triangles* in the corners.

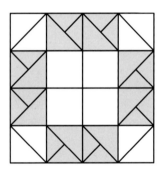

Instead of one middle unit, you have two. Draw the *Card Trick* component in both.

I could fill the center four squares with the same unit as the center square. But, after trying it, I felt the better path would be repeating the middle unit.

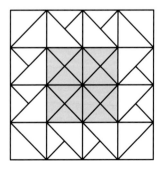

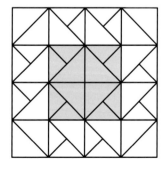

Trickies *centers*
Card Trick *units*

Card Trick *centers*
Card Trick *units*

Feel free to try other units in the center four squares. Here are a few that I tried with a four-patch Card Trick approach.

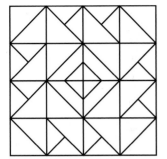 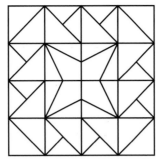 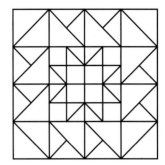

Half Night & Noon *center*   Ice Cream Cone II *center*   Wingy Things *center*

The next logical step was to take the expansion to a 5 x 5 grid. First fill in the corner units.

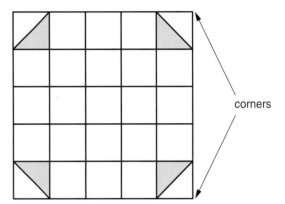

corners

Instead of one or two middle units, you now have three. Draw in the middle unit three times.

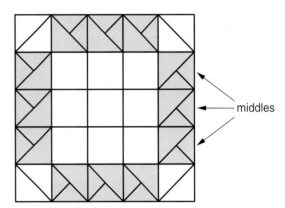

middles

What's left in the center is a nine-patch (3 x 3). So I put the original block into the center of the new five-patch.

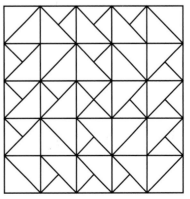

Card Trick expansion with
Card Trick center

Though it seemed logical to put the original block in the center, I thought it would be interesting to see what other blocks would look like.

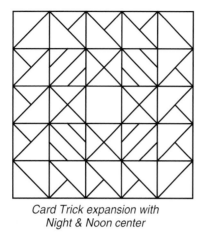

Card Trick expansion with
Night & Noon center

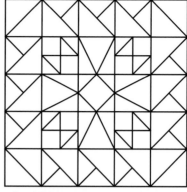

Card Trick expansion with Peaky &
Spike, Wingy Things, and
Center Diamond

Diversion

When I drew Card Trick as a five-patch, I realized that a five-patch was simply a nine-patch with a row of units around it. I'll come back to that thought when we continue designing five-patches. What I saw then was a flashback to my crocheting days and the ubiquitous granny square—a wonderful little unit like a quilt block. Instead of scrap fabric, the maker used scraps of yarn to make small squares that were sewn into a larger afghan. In the late 1960's and early 1970's, granny squares were revived. Every *Woman's Day* or *Family Circle* had 147 projects to do with the simple granny square: shower curtains, toaster covers, doggie jackets. One of the new interpretations was to make one giant granny square instead of a lot of little ones. The essence of the design was to turn the corner the same and increase the number of middle units with each round. Do you notice a similarity in terms? I did. Instead of settling for a five-patch Card Trick, I decided to continue expanding the Card Trick with concentric "rounds" of more *Card Trick* units with *Half-Square Triangle* corners. The first of these quilts was "Fond Memories of a Granny Square" (page 36) followed by "Win a Few, Lose a Few, 3 No Trump" (page 38).

The problem with the giant granny square and the giant Card Trick was that, if you start with a square, you end up with a square. If we could start with a rectangle, we could end up with a quilt or afghan that would fit a bed or a body. I first drew a rectangular grid. If I could construct a 3 x 3, 4 x 4, or 5 x 5 Card Trick, why not a 4 x 6 Card Trick? The first step was drawing the empty block. Then I put in corners. The sides have different numbers of middle units, but the scheme still works out.

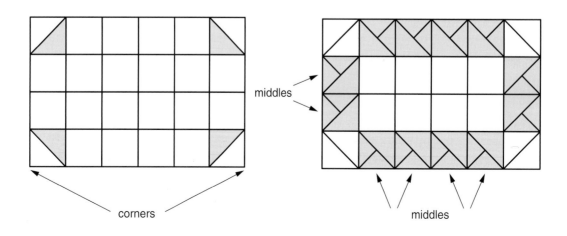

I dealt with the new rectangular center in the same way as the rest, with *Half-Square Triangles* in the corners and *Card Tricks* filling the middles.

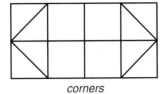

corners

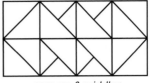

corners & middles

I could now use the 4 x 6 rectangular block as the core of a new granny square and follow with row after row. Because I started with a rectangle, I will end up with a rectangle. Two quilts that are completely different from each other started with the rectangle core: "Baby Card Trick" (page 36) and "Go Fish (Bassomatic)" (page 38). After having made all these quilts, I was casting around for another twist to the idea. This time I kept the Card Trick core but, instead of hundreds of *Card Trick* units, I used concentric rows of other block components. I made a wallhanging version: "Peaky & Spike and Friends" (page 40). By throwing a few borders between rows of units, I could bring it to quilt size. You can see how this is done in the projects in the back of this book.

Why do I bring this up now? Because I believe we all have creative surges that come from focusing on one design, and that we bring all of our experiences to quiltmaking. While you are working with the block components and creating new quilt blocks, you may be reminded of a sweater you knitted or wallpaper from your childhood room, or something I don't dare even imagine. Follow that idea. Spin it out with as many analogies as you can. This is why quiltmaking continues to hold my interest after years as a needlework enthusiast. I believe that what we have done gets us ready for what we are going to do. Let who you are and what you like show through in your quilts. I learned how to crochet in second grade and probably started playing cards (Old Maid, Go Fish, War) before that. Both these ideas surface in the Card Trick series of quilts.

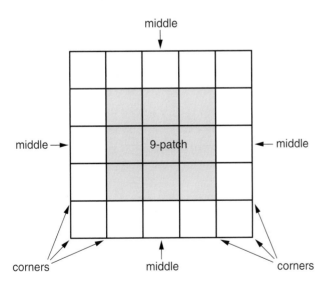

Method II (at last!): When I realized that a five-patch could be a nine-patch surrounded by another row of units, I used that as a new starting point. These adventures are great fun. With the five-patch, you have new middles and more corner. This method differs from the first because, now, I view the squares adjacent to the corners as additional corner squares, rather than as middle squares. You can start with a traditional block or one of your own nine-patches.

Set up at least four 5 x 5 grids. Choose a block for the center and draw it in. Look at the block components for middles, then corners, and draw them in.

What I look for in these blocks are new connections between outside units and the center. For example, when you put *Peaky & Spike* on top of *Peaky & Spike*, instead of two sets of points, you see an elongated chevron: watch how this will happen in the next example.

Here are a few examples of five-patch blocks that started with a nine-patch. Notice that one of your choices for outside middle is a plain *Square*. Look closely at these three blocks and analyze their similarities and differences. They are all variations on a theme, made up of basically the same components.

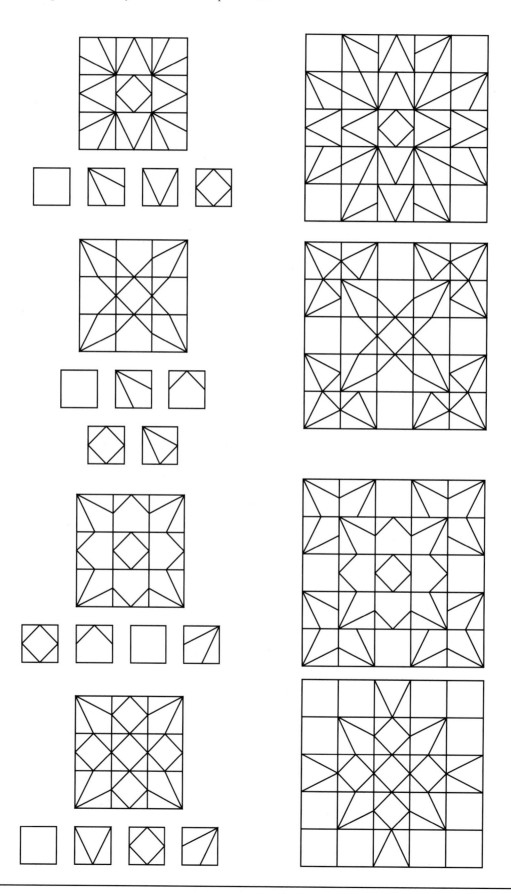

An inner nine-patch is created from *Center Diamond* center, *Peaky & Spike* middles, and *Wingy Thing* corners, surrounded by *Trickies* and *Half-Square Triangles*, and *Square* corners. This block was used in "Office Quilt" (page125) and a variation became "Peaky and Spike Go to Africa" (page 78 and page 128).

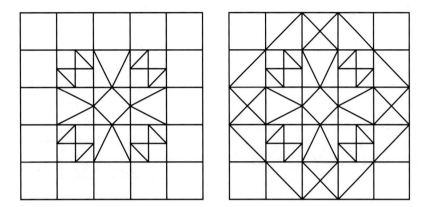

Method III: This approach to creating a 5 x 5 block starts by looking at the five-patch in another way. Instead of a nine-patch with a row around, we can also see it as crossbars with four-patch corners.

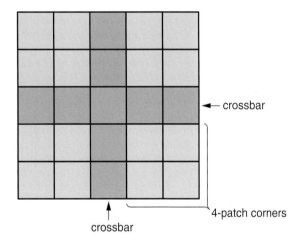

Crossbars can be created by stringing components together. One of my favorites is *Peaky & Spike* on top of *Peaky & Spike* or facing each other.

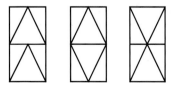

Other possibilities for crossbars are *Flying Geese,* or *Flying Geese* and *Peaky & Spike,* or *Chevron-Rectangle-Flying Geese.*

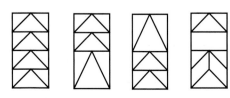

Now look for a four-patch to fill in the corners. Again the possibilities are endless, but here are a few examples. I loved the lily block created from *Mutt & Jeff* and *Ice Cream Cones II*. From it I could take the four-patch essence of the lily.

 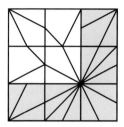

I put the four-patch lily in the corners of the 5 x 5 block, then looked for crossbars and a center. I chose a double *Peaky & Spike* for crossbars and *Center Diamond* for the center.

  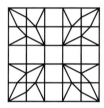 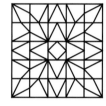

You can now flip those units so that they point in a different direction. Some other 5 x 5's created with crossbars and four-patches follow.

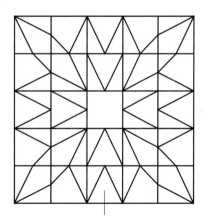

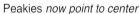
Peakies *now point to center*

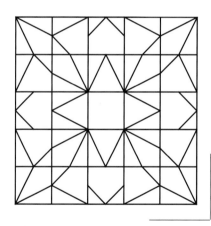

lilies point in
instead of out

crossbar

corners

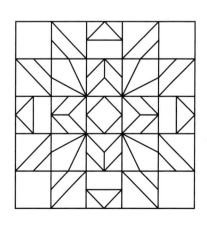

Here is a *Center Diamond* center, middles created from *Chevrons*, *Rectangle*, and *Flying Geese*, corners of *Ice Cream Cone II, Half Night & Noon,* and *Square*. This block is used in "Ambrosia" (page 99).

22

Now a *Center Diamond* center, *Peaky & Spike* middles, *Ice Cream Cones II* corners and *Four-Patches*. This block was used in "St. Elsewhere" (page 121) and "Gulessarian Stars" (page 126).

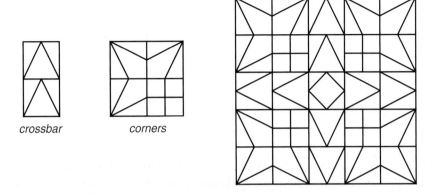

crossbar   corners

Here are two more examples of blocks created with Method III.

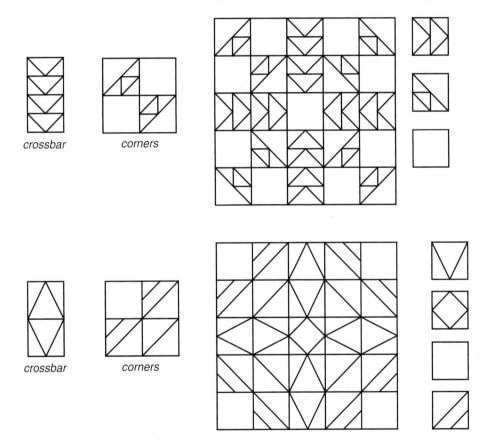

crossbar   corners

crossbar   corners

I've been playing around with some other approaches to designing quilt blocks. The method is really the same but, instead of single units or components, we can use four-patches as components. I used the lily shape in five-patches. These blocks were used in "Cross Street Pasture," "Bahamian Blossoms," and "Cheap Trick" (pages 103 and 104). But I wasn't finished with the lily. So this time I used the lily four-patch as an element of a larger nine-patch in the small Lily quilts (pages 34 and 35) and "Flower Dung Song" (page 33).

lily four-patch

corners

center

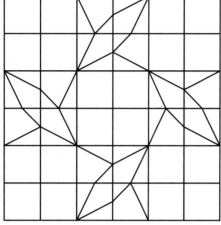

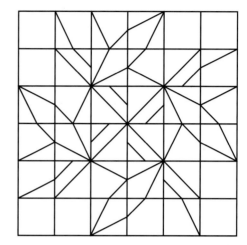

lilies in middle position

I <u>still</u> wasn't finished with the lily, so this time I pushed four of them together into a four-patch block. The block itself is great, but I added a row around it in the same way we can turn a nine-patch into a five-patch. I used this block in the quilt called "Prickly Itch" (page 37).

lily four-patch

4 lilies together

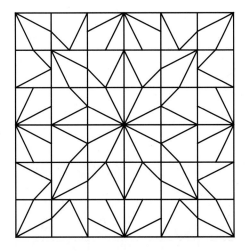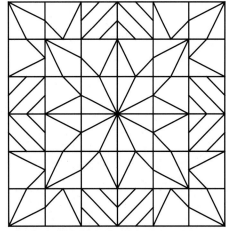

block used in "Prickly Itch"

I have described and illustrated many different approaches to designing quilt blocks. Although materials on a printed page have to appear in some sort of order, one line after the next, you will realize that the creative process is not always so orderly or linear. Once you start working with the components, you will find your ideas flowing and overflowing in many directions. But they won't flow at all if you don't put pen to paper: the best way to understand and to learn is to DO. Then let your ideas from one block lead on to another and another. And have fun!

QUILT DESIGN

Designing quilt blocks is great fun. But, unless we want pillows stacked from floor to ceiling or more tote bags than we have things to tote, it's time to explore quilt design—the arrangement of blocks to make a quilt or wallhanging. We can look to quilts from the past for examples and still create quilts that are innovative. Experiment with all the methods, and your ideas will begin to flow.

BLOCK-TO-BLOCK

One of the simplest ideas that can lead to interesting and seemingly complex quilts is block-to-block setting. Blocks are put together with no sashing or setting strips (different words for the same thing). We might be tempted to dismiss this setting as predictable if we view each block as a separate design, by itself: the resulting quilt could look like row upon row of pillow tops. But, if we think of the quilt block, like the components that make up that block, as part of a larger design, we can create new ideas for quilts.

To see what I mean, look at these examples. Each block was created with essentially the same components: *Peaky & Spike* and *Night & Noon* with a *Pinwheel* or *Center Diamond* in the center. Look at the plain black-and-white line drawings, then at the shaded versions. Make a copy and color some for yourself. Look for the new designs created at block sides and corners. Are there any new design elements visible in the all-over drawing that are not evident in the single block? Can you do something with the background to add depth? I try to think of what would be predictable, and then I do something different.

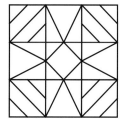
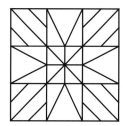
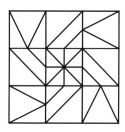

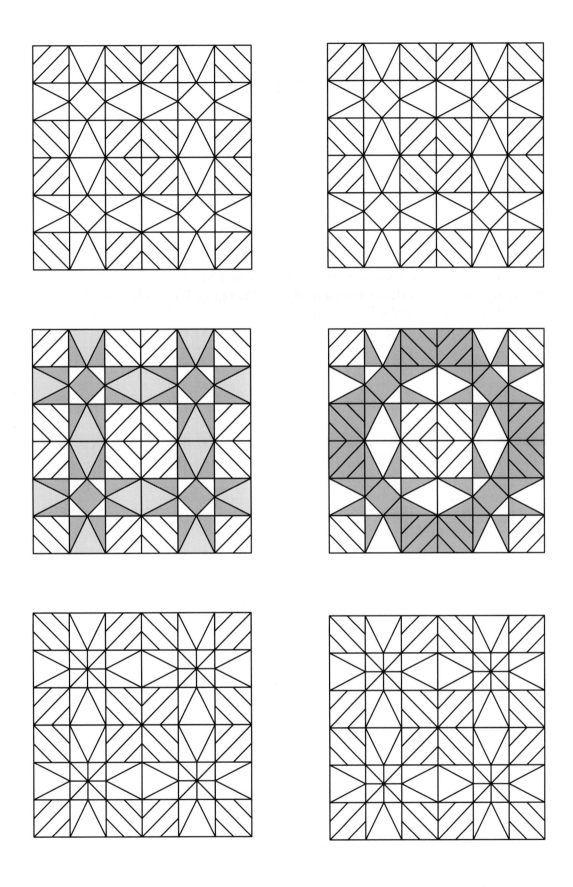

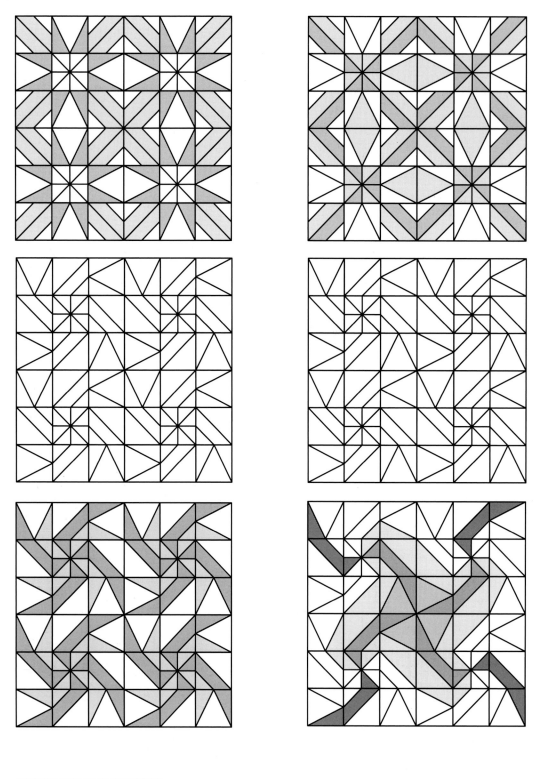

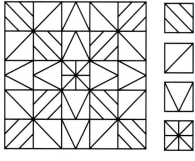

Lets look at a few more examples. The rust and blue quilt on page 39 is another variation of the *Peaky & Spike* with *Night & Noon* combination, this time as a five-patch block. When the blocks are set together, a new design appears at the corners. By shifting the background colors, we see a small square and a larger square on point.

The "Heart" quilt series is an excellent example of block-to-block setting, showing how one idea can lead to another. The original block was created from *Peaky & Spike* middles, *Half-Square Triangle* corners, and a *Center Diamond* center. When these blocks are set together, we can isolate many different design elements—if we ignore block boundaries and look instead for bigger shapes. This drawing is a doodle, not a finished quilt design. In it, you can see all kinds of possibilities: an eight-pointed star, circles, ogees, diagonal ribbons, hearts. (I was thrilled that I could piece a heart without sewing a curved seam!) The first quilt in the series was "Hearts of Space" (page 58). My approach to color was to define the hearts by making them in a variety of solid reds and pinks, set against teal background prints. The relative values of the reds and teals are very close, thus the subtitle "Ultimate Test for Red-Green Color Blindness."

Now you play!

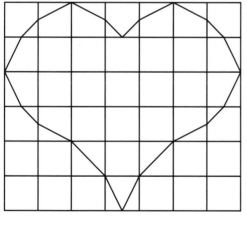

I loved fooling around with the hearts, and I could have made more versions of the original. Instead, I next erased all the lines except those creating the grid and the outer edge of the heart. Now, with empty space to deal with, I could change the design significantly. A nine-patch block fits perfectly inside the heart. I could foresee a quilting problem if I left the nine-patch sitting isolated in the middle, so I softened the edges with what looks like a circle with pointed bumps.

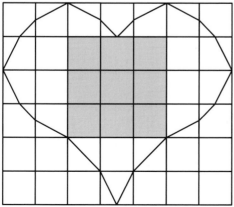

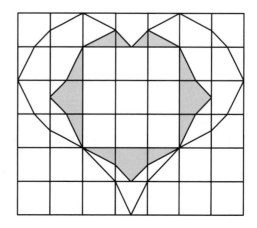

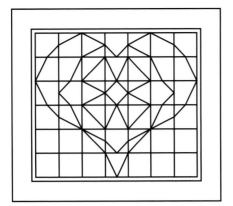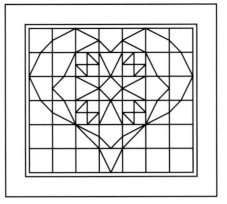

The transition from block to heart is now more graceful, the circle smoothing the sharp edges of the block. These new hearts can be used singly as blocks (page 57), or they can be linked into horizontal rows, as in "Czech Hearts." The center of each heart contains a nine-patch created from *Ice Cream Cones* and *Center Diamonds*.

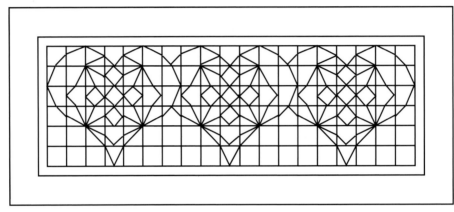

This idea next led me to thinking of the hearts as a new setting for sampler blocks. In "My Heart Belongs to Quilting" on page 58, four rows of three hearts each are set together. A different nine-patch block is set into the middle of each heart and surrounded by the circular effect.

Flower Dung Song
100" x 68"
hand quilted

All fabrics are 100% cotton, and all quilts are machine pieced.

African Lily
40" x 40"
unquilted top

Night Garden
36" x 36"
unquilted top

Mini Lilies
20" x 20"
unquilted top

Peach Lilies
32" x 32"
hand quilted

Neon Lilies
33" x 33"
hand quilted

Magpie Road Kill
40" x 40"
hand quilted

Baby Card Trick
47" x 38½"
hand quilted

Fond Memories of a Granny Square
64" x 64"
hand quilted

Daisy Deals Devon
30" x 30"
unquilted top

Mary's Card Trick
28" x 28"
hand quilted
Collection of Mary Stori

Prickly Itch
55" x 55"
hand quilted

see pg 155

Go Fish (Bassomatic)
46" x 38"
unquilted top

Win a Few, Lose a Few,
3 No Trump
43" x 43"
unquilted top

Harold's Quilt
104" x 84"
hand quilted by the author and machine quilted by Dalene Young Thomas
Collection of Harold Nadel

see
pg 145

Project
Peaky & Spike and Friends
58" x 48"
hand quilted

Cow Quilt
(Picowsoos with Mootisse Border)
28" x 28"
hand quilted

When *Quilter's Newsletter Magazine* asked me to design a new series quilt in 1992, I returned to the "Heart" quilts. When I eliminated the hearts, I was left with the pointy circles surrounding different nine-patch blocks. To make it even more interesting, I broke up the background into small scrap squares (page 60). All this explanation shows you not only how the "Heart" quilts developed but also how you can work within the grid to eliminate some designs and add others.

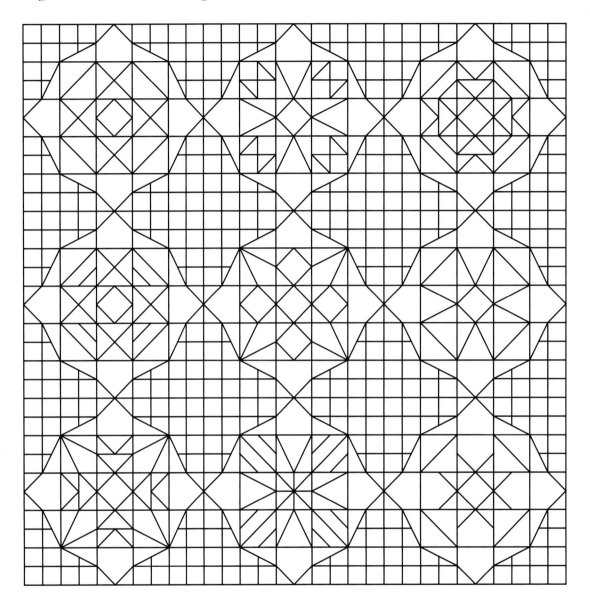

Try it for yourself. First draw a traditional block, or repeat one you created in the preceding chapter. Fill a page with that same block, setting each block side by side and row by row. Make copies of it before you start to color in, so you won't have to re-draw it when you want to try a different color configuration. Get out the colored pencils and color it in the way you first visualized the block. The second time, look at where the corners of the blocks come together as the center of a new design. Try it one more time, looking for all-over lines that run from one block to the other. Eliminate lines that don't add anything to the design, or add lines to help carry through an idea. This how a series is born.

We can take the process of block-to-block settings a step farther. By erasing parts of the block or rearranging the block itself, we can create some truly original quilts. For example, follow me through the design process for "Blessed Relief" (page 64).

The original is a 4 x 4 grid, and the components have some twists: *Ice Cream Cones I,* *Squares* <u>*with a corner removed*</u>, and *Wingy Things* <u>*minus one Wingy*</u>.

I divided the block in half and put the halves together backward. These new blocks were placed in the middle positions around the original block, creating the effect of a medallion in the center where the edges of the semicircles touch.

The corner blocks are the original block with one quarter of each replaced by a plain square. Although this is basically a nine-block quilt, the overall effect is of a medallion surrounded by a border of partial blocks.

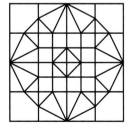
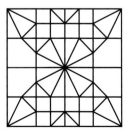
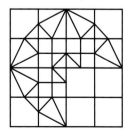

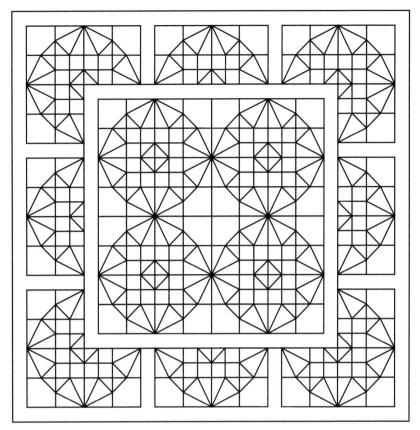

In the next design adventure, the same block is repeated four times in the center, then separated from the border blocks by sashing. The idea is then expanded with nine blocks in the center of the quilt, and half-blocks are offset on the sides.

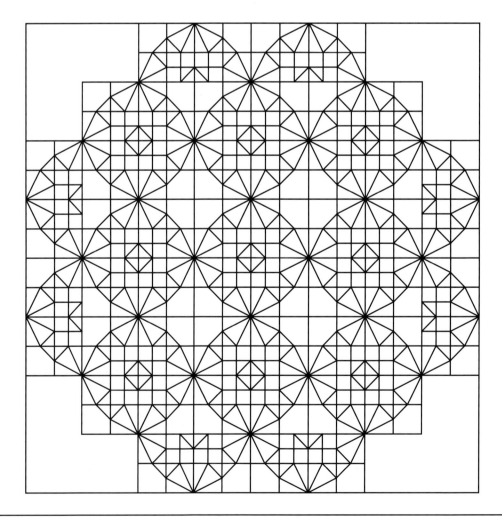

I loved the idea of working with partial blocks. In "July" (page 60) I started with a full block on the left. I wanted it to look like a bouncing beach ball, so the successive blocks are partially concealed behind the first block. The effect is one of layering, although the layering happened in the designing, not the sewing. I made six copies of the block and cut them out, then laid them on graph paper, moving them around to see the sizes of the empty spaces.

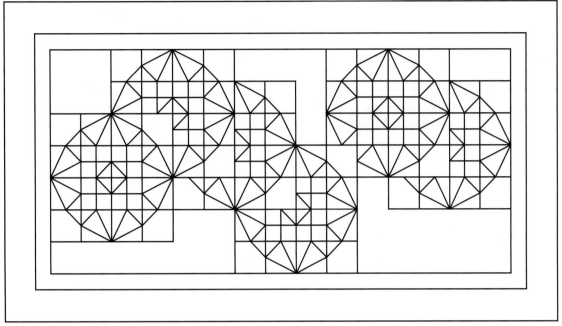

"July"

To try this for yourself, choose one of your four-patch blocks, since they are the easiest to cut in half or quarters. Make copies of your choice. Cut them apart. Then rearrange the blocks so they overlap. You will find this easier to manipulate if you place the pieces on graph paper.

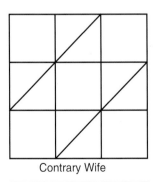

Contrary Wife

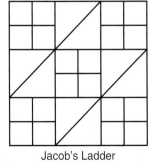

Jacob's Ladder

DIRECTIONAL BLOCK-TO-BLOCK SETTINGS

Worlds of new patterning are opened to us when we use directional blocks in block-to-block settings. Directional blocks have a strong visual line that runs diagonally from one corner to another. The simplest of these is Contrary Wife, which has *Half-Square Triangles* in the middles.

With the addition of *Four-Patches* in the corners and center, the block is called Jacob's Ladder. By adding new components to the center and corners, we can create new directional blocks. These blocks don't always look great just sitting there as nine-patches; they come to life only in a setting.

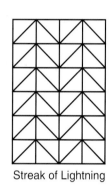

Quilter's Newsletter Magazine #116, many years ago, featured Log Cabin quilts. At that moment I realized Log Cabin quilts work the way they do because of the strong diagonal line created by light and dark sides. Traditional Log Cabins could be arranged in several ways: Barn Raising, Straight Furrows, Sunshine & Shadow, and Streak of Lightning are the most familiar.

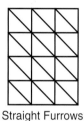

Straight Furrows

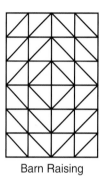

Barn Raising

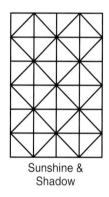

Sunshine &
Shadow

Streak of Lightning

We can use these same settings with directional blocks. The results can be very interesting, because the blocks have more than just a strong diagonal line; there is often a counterpoint pattern. For example, here is a block created with *Half-Square Triangles* in the middles and *Night & Noons* in opposite corners and the center. On its own this looks like a pretty drippy block. Arranged in traditional Log Cabin settings, the block takes on a new personality.

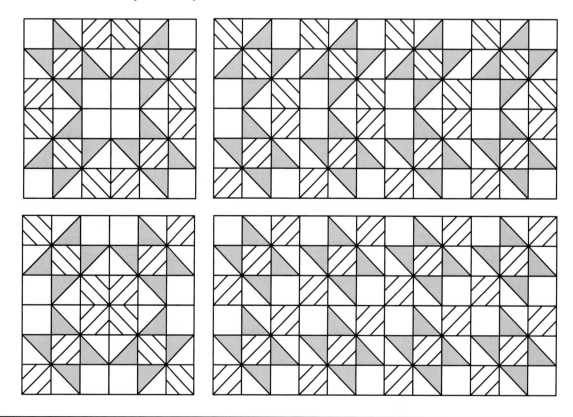

Barn Raising

Let's look at some other blocks in traditional settings. These start with *Half-Square Triangle* middles and *Wingy Things.* See this block in Barn Raising set and in Streak of Lightning set.

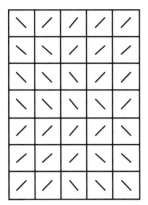

Arrangement of diagonals for
"Running Hot and Cold"

A quilt I had a great time making in a non-traditional arrangement is "Running Hot and Cold" (page 61). The block has *Half Night & Noon* middles and *Four-Patches*. Because I almost always work symmetrically, I wanted to try something different. I suppose we could call it a Straight Furrow that couldn't make up its mind. The quilt is effective because the cool squares keep marching through the warm area, and warm squares radiate through the cool area.

"Running Hot and Cold"

The point with all of these examples is to show the potential of working with directional blocks. I think I have only scratched the surface. The designs become more complicated when you have more blocks to work with. Try some for yourself. Probably the easiest way to do that is with blocks copied and cut out, as suggested above. That way you can try all of the possibilities, from the traditional to the offbeat.

Diagonal or directional blocks can be based on units other than *Half-Square Triangles*. We can use *Ice Cream Cones* and *Mutt & Jeffs* to get the same effect.

As an exercise, I tried each of the blocks in traditional four-block settings: Barn Raising, Sunshine & Shadow, and Straight Furrows. Straight Furrows often appears to be the least effective of the settings, yet there are hints of great things in some of the blocks.

Barn Raising   Sunshine & Shadow   Straight Furrows

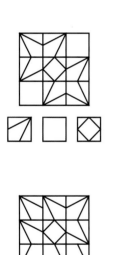 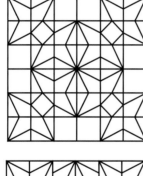 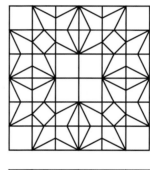 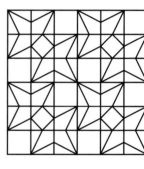

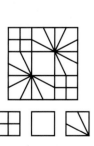 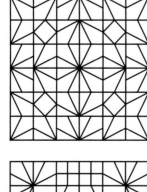 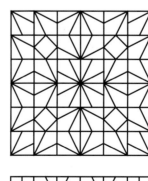 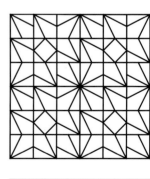

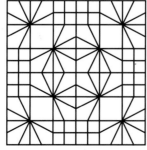 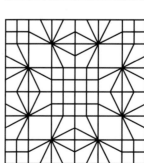 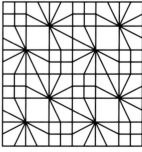

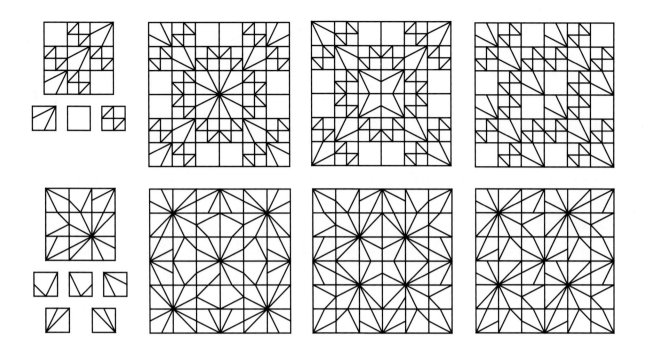

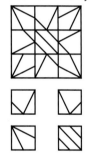

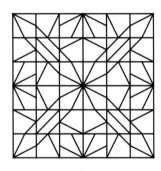

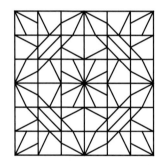

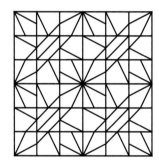

After experimenting with the block in all the configurations, I was fascinated by the circle in the center, with what appear to be diagonal blades on top.

"Good and Plenty"

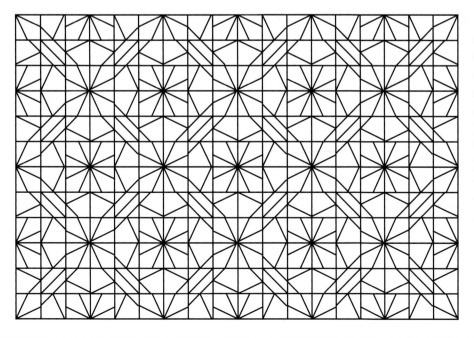

When additional sets of four blocks are put together, another circle is created. This design became "Good and Plenty" (page 63). The more blocks we have to work with, the more complex the design can become.

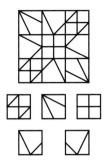

I tried yet another of the directional blocks, using *Ice Cream Cones I, Mutt & Jeffs, Four-Patch,* and *Wingy Things.* I liked the opposing diagonals created with squares and triangles marching opposite to the cones and *Mutt & Jeffs.* The blocks looked good in Barn Raising and Sunshine & Shadows, and even Straight Furrows showed potential.

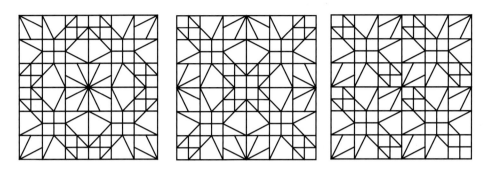

I tried one more layout: Streak of Lightning. I placed the hot colors (red, orange, yellow) to run through the small squares and triangles, and cool colors (blue, green, violet) were assigned to the *Ice Cream Cones I* and the peaky side of *Mutt & Jeffs.* The result is "Electric Slide" (page 64).

"Electric Slide"

Another directional block that has been great fun to play around with starts with *Peaky & Spike*. Three corners are *Half Night & Noon* and the center is a whole *Night and Noon*.

 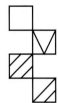

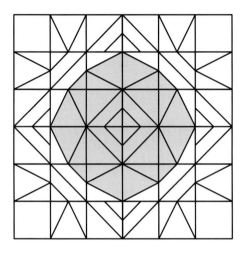

When we put four blocks together in the Barn Raising setting, the overall design is of a round peg in a square hole. The center circle is enclosed and surrounded by squares on point. There's opportunity to use more than one background fabric, and a border print. The first of these I called "Aerial View." I loved the design so much, I've taught it for years as "Stormy Sea Wallhanging" (pages 59 and 62).

I redesigned the center of the quilt, replacing the yellow area with *Ice Cream Cones I* and *Spike*. Although the corners didn't change, for the first time I saw the corner four-patch as a fish, not just *Peaky & Spike* and *Night & Noon*. (We'll come back to the fish later.)

I wanted to enlarge the four-block design but did not want something that looked like a bunch of wallhangings sewn together. I first made copies of the original. One I left whole and pasted down in the middle of the page. A second copy I cut in half and placed above and below, and a third left and right. The fourth original is cut into the basic nine-patches and used to fill in the corners. To make the quilt rectangular, repeat the last row. The result was a Barn Raising setting, arrived at from another direction. The final design looked to me like much more than a sum of its parts. New shapes that weren't evident in the original come out when more blocks are set together. The teal three-quarter-circle actually starts in what was background of the original four-block.

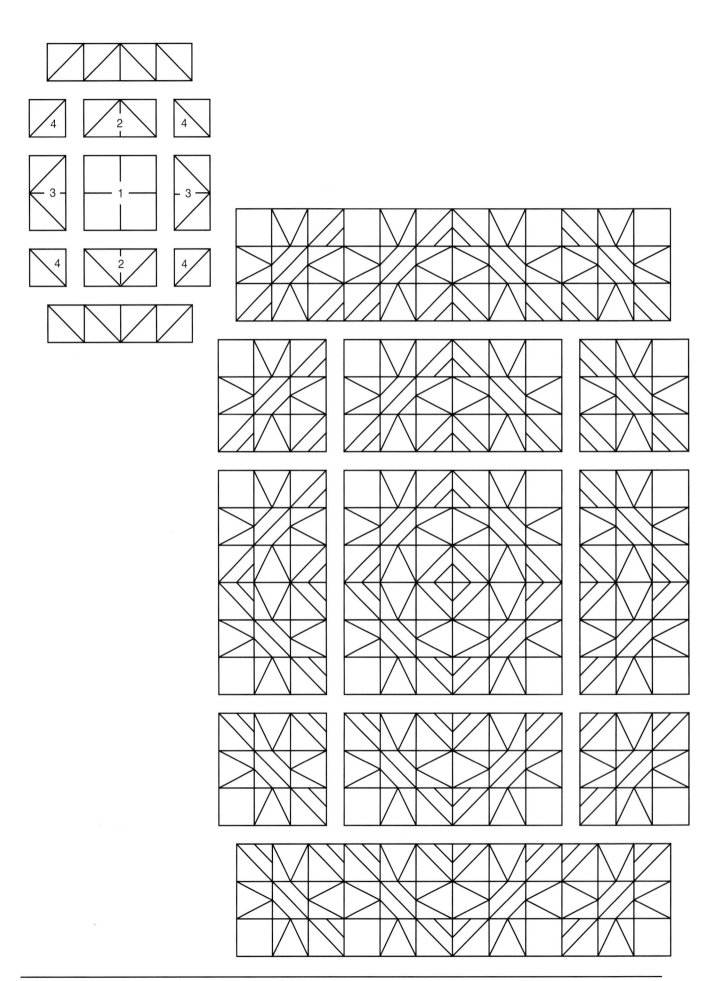

"Eye of the Storm"

Now back to the fish. They could be liberated from the quilt and used as an independent four-patch. By a change of scale we can have big fish and little fish in the same quilt. A symmetrical treatment of the fish would be to plug them into a 5 x 5 block: four-patch corners with crossbars (page 62).

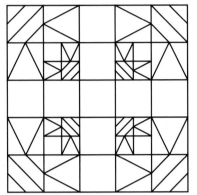 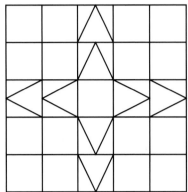 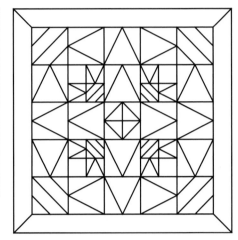

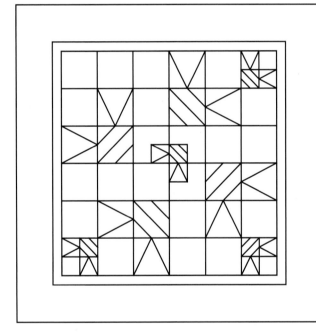

In a real departure from my symmetrical self, I turned the fish loose to swim where they pleased. This is one of the quilting cruise projects (page 62).

ALTERNATE BLOCK SETTING

Another setting choice is also block-to-block but, instead of the same block repeated over and over, we can work with different blocks. This is certainly not an original idea to quiltmaking, but it is a great way to create new quilt images from familiar patterns.

I hadn't seen all those existing multiple-block quilts when it occurred to me that I could arrange quilt blocks like components in a nine-patch. The first possibility is working with traditional blocks, straight out of a book. We can do this with either two or three different blocks, placing block #1 in the center, four block #2's in the middles, and four block #3's in the corners, or we can repeat block #1 in the corners.

3	2	3
2	1	2
3	2	3

Purple Heart
28" x 30"
machine quilted

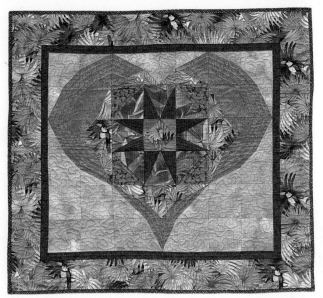

Green Heart
25" x 28"
machine quilted

Czech Hearts
25" x 65"
hand quilted

Pink Hearts
47" x 54"
unquilted top

Hearts of Space (Ultimate Test for Red-Green Color Blindness)
62" x 66"
hand quilted

My Heart Belongs to Quilting
106" x 86"
unquilted top

Aerial View
33" x 33"
hand quilted

Stormy Sea Pink
34" x 34"
unquilted top

Stormy Sea Navy
35" x 35"
machine quilted

Stormy Sea
30" x 30"
hand quilted

Lace Circles
61" x 61"
unquilted top

July
40" x 72"
hand quilted
Collection of
Paul Pilgrim and
Gerald Roy

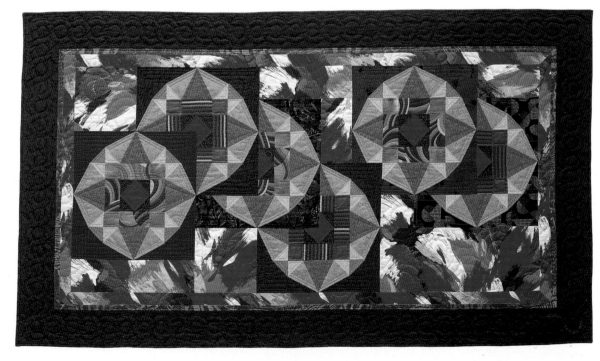

Running Hot and Cold
90" x 66"
unquilted top

Discovery Fish
31" x 31"
unquilted top

Stormy Sea Challenge
24" x 24"
hand quilted

Liberated Fish
31½" x 31½"
hand quilted

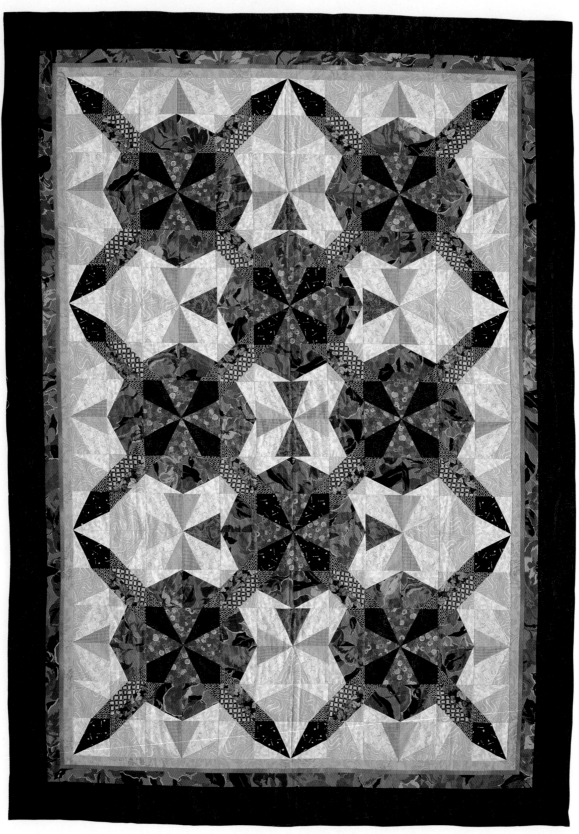

Good and Plenty
83" x 60"
unquilted top

Blessed Relief
58" x 58"
unquilted top

Electric Slide
93" x 68"
unquilted top

What I look for in choosing the blocks is that they be on the same grid system: nine-patches with nine-patches or five-patches with five-patches. That way, lines can start in one block and continue uninterrupted into another. One of the simplest of these combinations I tried was Ohio Star alternating with *Peaky & Spike* with corners in "Amanda's Quilt" (page 97).

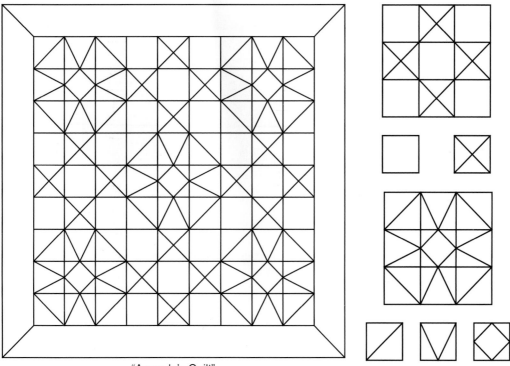

"Amanda's Quilt"

Storm at Sea

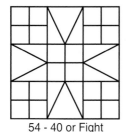

54 - 40 or Fight

California Sunset
(J. Beyer)

As you can see in "Amanda's Quilt," the visual effect is simple: two different stars floating on the same background. A few years later, as I prepared for a teaching trip to Australia, I decided to make a quilt with koalas and kangaroos to use as my autograph hound (Does that date me?). The simplicity of piecing made "Amanda's Quilt" a perfect candidate for repetition. "Peaky & Spike Go to Australia" (page 98) is "Amanda's Quilt" with a new color focus. In these block combinations, you have to do your best to forget what the blocks look like on their own. Then it is possible to see the square on point around the peaky star. The curved sections on the outside of the strong green diagonal were a complete surprise.

"Butter Churn" (page 103) is another block-combination wallhanging from three traditional blocks. I made the selection by turning to page 70 of Jinny Beyer's *Quilter's Album of Blocks and Borders*. I chose California Sunset for the center block for one reason: it was the hardest piece, and I had to make only one. Storm at Sea is in the middle positions and 54-40 or Fight in the corners. In the black-and-white bare-bones drawing, I see all kinds of possibilities. Besides the obvious eight-pointed *Peaky* stars, there are four large diamonds and squares that march from corners into the center. (Some viewers see what look like curvy propeller blades first.)

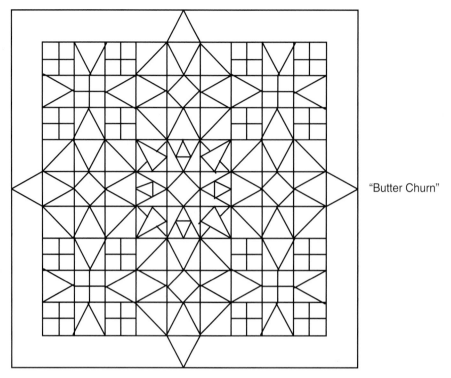

"Butter Churn"

I guess I could have continued to work with traditional blocks forever. But I wanted to try using original blocks with traditional, or even all original, blocks. If some blocks regularly lose their identity to the whole, it seemed reasonable to create new blocks especially for the quilt. It makes for some odd, very un-pillow-like blocks. In "Peaky & Spike Go to the Grand Caymans" (page 99), I took the same four blocks we used in "Stormy Sea Wallhanging" and placed them in the four corners. The center block is *Peaky & Spike* with *Half Night & Noon* corners. The middle blocks are *Peaky & Spikes* with a *Chevron* and *Half Night & Noons*. Look also at "Christmas Rose" (page 102) and "Antipasto" (page 67) for other examples of the same approach.

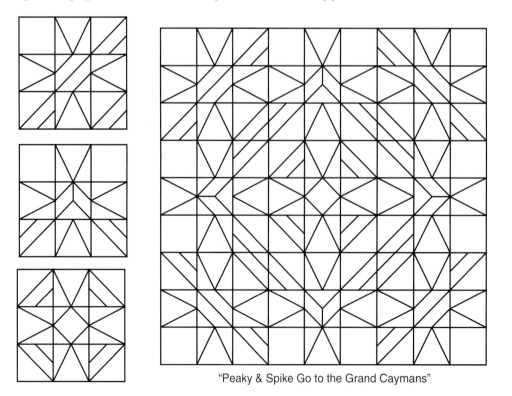

"Peaky & Spike Go to the Grand Caymans"

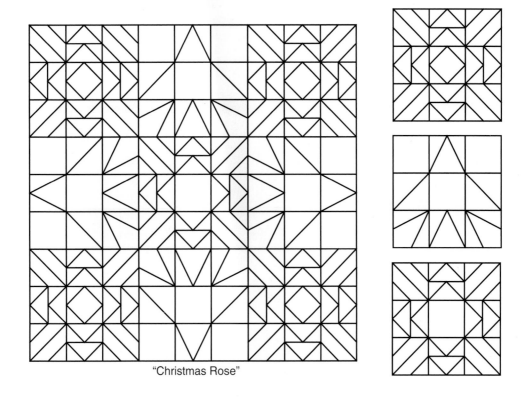

"Christmas Rose"

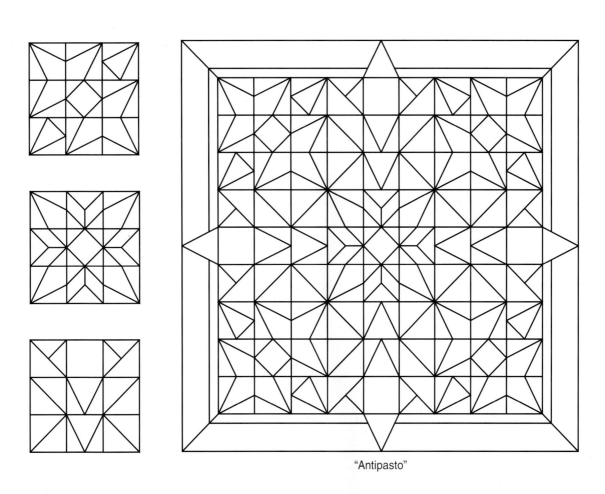

"Antipasto"

3	2	3
2	1	2
M 3	2	M 3
2	1	2
3	2	1

The problem I had with this idea was that the best designs turned out to be suitable for small square wallhangings. Who has that many walls? We can expand from the nine-block trap easily by working with unsymmetrical numbers of blocks. From 3 x 3 blocks, I first tried 3 x 5 blocks. "Sally's Stars" (page 101) is the enlarged version of "Butter Churn." I modified the 54-40 or Fight block in the middles so the squares could march in both directions. Notice that blocks #2 and #3 are simplified from "Butter Churn."

"Sally's Stars"

In alternating block designs, we have the <u>potential</u> for crossover from one block to another; <u>color</u> makes it a reality. Try to look at your design as a whole, and not as individual blocks. This might mean that what could be a point to a star in a single block is now part of the background. The best way to learn this is to make copies of some of the line drawings, then attack them with colored pencils. What excites me about these designs is the potential for visual complexity. I'm thrilled when there appear to be layers of design. In other words, I love it when I haven't seen everything in the quilt at first glance.

SETTING BLOCKS TOGETHER WITH STRIPS

Our next option, after block-to-block setting, is to separate the blocks with setting or sashing strips. In this time-honored way of putting a quilt together, the strips simply separate one block from another and keep their edges from touching. The setting strip with setting square is also the basis of more complicated setting options such as checkerboard and garden maze, which make it possible to create new designs which center upon the setting square. With even the simplest setting option, we can vary the width of the strips, and we can create contrast with the block for some interesting effects.

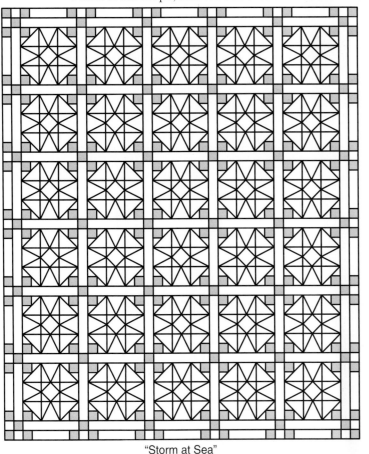

"Storm at Sea"

If necessary, sashing also will increase the size of the quilt and make fewer blocks go farther: more quilt with less piecing. Let's look at a few examples; later we'll look at the technical details.

In "Ambrosia" (page 99) I hadn't planned to use setting strips at all. Size wasn't a problem, because the quilt top with blocks alone already measured 60" x 80". But, when the corners of four blocks came together, there was just a big white blob. Simple narrow sashing divided the blocks enough to separate the corners. I used simple sashing again in "Cheap Trick" (page 103), this time for a completely different reason: I was fairly certain that I wanted to use the border fabric, and I thought it would look too tacked-on if I didn't introduce it somewhere within the quilt. Because the blocks were already sewn, the logical place to introduce it was in setting strips. A third quilt using a simple setting with setting square is "Storm at Sea" (page 97). The same quilt layout could be colored so it would simply look like nine-patch Storm at Sea blocks divided by setting strips. By matching the fabric of the setting strips to triangles in the block, and the setting square to the corner squares, I created the effect of red nine-patches alternating with pointy stars in octagons; again we find unexpected designs.

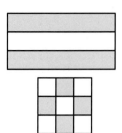

The idea of new designs at the setting squares intrigued me, so I looked to other traditional settings for more ideas. A classic is the checkerboard, dividing the setting strips into three stripes. The setting square is a small nine-patch in the same two fabrics with light fabric in the corner squares. The result is a very strong setting that separates the blocks and, because of its size, can increase the dimensions of the quilt considerably.

We can put a few new twists on the traditional checkerboard. One idea I think is great but haven't tried is to use scraps for the strips and checkerboard. It would be a great way to sew up leftover strips and could tie a diverse group of blocks together.

Another approach is to look at the checkerboard setting square as an extension of the block itself. (Here's where it is fun to be able to design your own blocks!) I took a five-patch block, designed earlier, and added four-patch units in the corners.

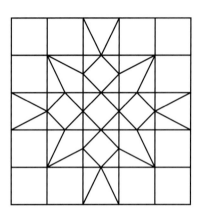
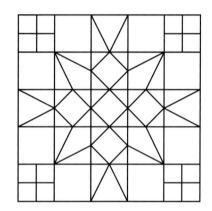

If we set this into a checkerboard setting and scale it so the size of the setting squares matches the four-patch, we have some interesting possibilities for marching color diagonally through the quilt. The three-stripe sashing could be made a strong contrast to the edges of the block, or a more subtle shift of background.

This is probably a good time to talk about scale. Generally, I want the width of the strips and the size of the checkerboard to be compatible with the block. (Inappropriate extremes would be 1½" total of strips with a 20" block or 4½" with a 6" block.) For blocks from 12" to 16", I would work with three 1" strips; for larger blocks, perhaps 1½" strips. For blocks under 12", I would consider strips from ½" to ¾" (thus total width less than 2½") more proportionally pleasing.

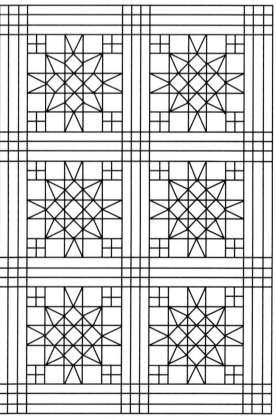

"Checkerboard"

This assumes that all the strips and squares in the nine-patch need to be the same size. In "Bahamian Blossoms" (page 103), I thought an equal amount of pink and blue would be too pink, so I narrowed the pink and widened the blue. This altered the look of the checkerboard as well.

"Cross Street Pasture" (page 104) (the same block as "Cheap Trick" and "Bahamian Blossoms") uses another variation of this setting. Now, in the sashing, the two outside strips are narrowed and the center is enlarged. A checkerboard setting square could have been used, but I put in a center diamond instead.

You could question whether or not this is even a checkerboard setting, but in my mind it is because of how I derived it. That to me is the essence of creativity: getting so far from the source that it is unrecognizable. <u>I see traditional forms as the launching pad for new ideas, instead of as rules that must be adhered to.</u>

Designs at the Setting Square

We can take the concept of piecing in the sashing and in the setting square a bit further. Inspired by the accidental nine-patch and the piecing of the checkerboard in "Storm at Sea" (page 97), I looked at the setting square as the center of a new nine-patch; the width of the setting strip determines the size of the new block. Storm at Sea can be changed ever so slightly when we add a square to either end of the setting strips, page 103.

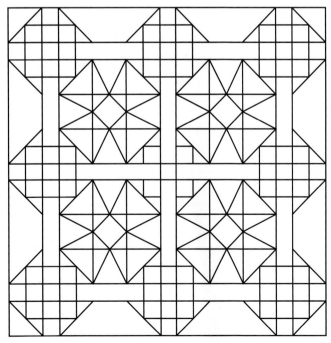

"Storm at Sea with Churn Dash"

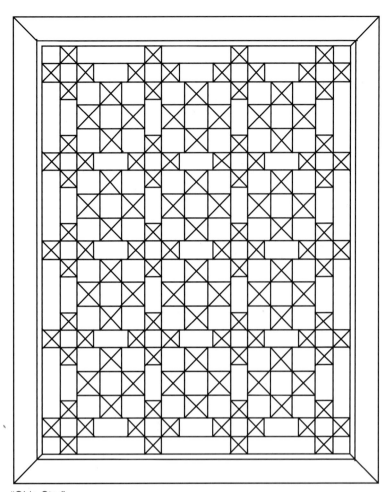

"Ohio Star"

The "Ohio Star" (page 98) and "Double Peaky & Spike" were developed by making new lines or adding piecing to the setting strips. By sewing *Trickies* at the ends of the strips, we get miniature Ohio Stars whose centers are the setting squares. I added small *Peakies* to the ends of the setting strips and pieced a *Center Diamond* in the setting square in "Double Peaky & Spike." In each case, the setting strip is narrower than a unit in the block; the new block is smaller than the original. In these quilts, I haven't intruded into the original blocks; all the design happens in the setting strips.

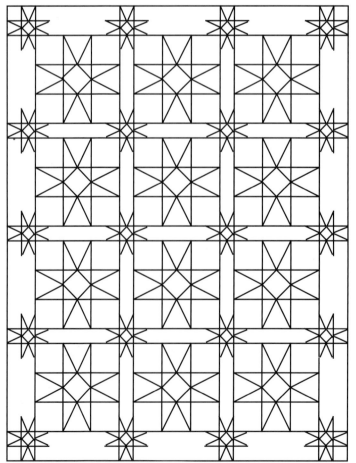

"Double Peaky & Spike"

We can expand the idea by letting the new little block overlap the larger original. In "Churn Dash Variation," the corner triangles of the tiny Churn Dashes are a part of the corner squares of the big Churn Dashes. When that setting strip is half the width of a block unit, that corner unit will in fact be a *Half Night & Noon*. Staying in a traditional vein, we could combine a variety of big and little blocks. Try some for yourself: Ohio Star with Churn Dash, Weathervane with Ohio Star, Churn Dash with Storm at Sea. Then work with some of your original blocks in combination with the traditional.

"Churn Dash Variation"

I thought it would be interesting to try my surprise block "short-legged long-legged it-looks-like-a-drafting-nightmare-but-it's-just-a-nine-patch" star. (I think I need a new name for that!) I drew four big blocks on paper with solid sashing. The proportion this time is different: a 9" block combined with a 6" setting block. In the big blocks, the *Ice Cream Cones* spin in one direction, while the little *Ice Cream Cones* spin the opposite way. To make the line from the top of the 2" triangle to the top of the of the peaky, I had to piece into the corner of the big block. The "Topsy-Turvy" quilt (page 122) looks as if the stars are kind of set on point and floating on a big beige background.

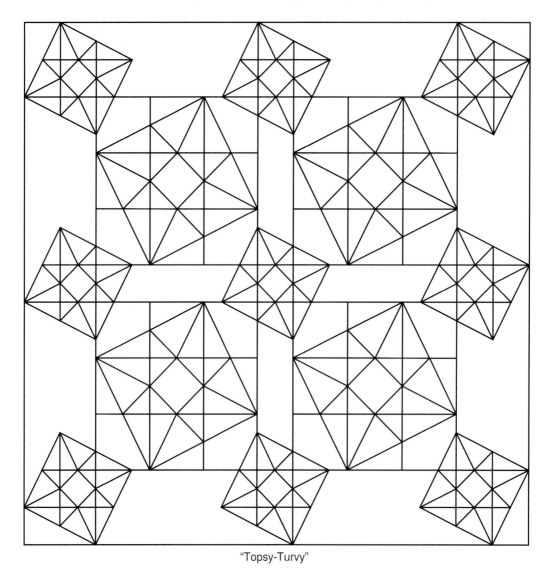

"Topsy-Turvy"

To see how very much fun this is, try a few for yourself. You can use the simple sashing layout sheet. Make copies of 1½" blocks. Cut and glue them into the large block spaces. Now look at the setting square as the center of a new nine-patch. Do the corners of the big block contribute an element for the little block? Can you make the new design by just piecing into the setting strip, or do you need to add lines to the original block? Play!

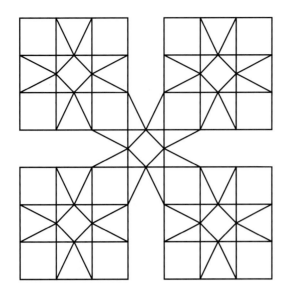

Full-Width Setting Strips

As long as the strips between the blocks are narrower than the units in the block, the new design at the setting square will be smaller than the original block. If we make the setting strip the same width as a unit in the block, we won't be able to see where the individual elements begin and end. I experimented with a few simple ideas at first. When the setting strips are the same width as a unit, note that the *Peaky* in the setting meets the *Peaky* in the block, creating a continuous line. If we expand this to full-quilt size, we can find the same great shapes as we did in block-to-block settings. (See page 29.)

When we look at the finished quilt "Peaky & Spike with Night & Noon" (page 128), it is hard to tell which is the block and which is the setting because of the common corners. Look at the line drawing. The touching *Peakies* create a curve that reminds me of a Double Wedding Ring quilt.

With any of these designs, you have to decide how to finish the quilt. If you stop with the first sashing, the new design will be only two-thirds there; you need another row of units to complete the pattern. That will become obvious as you draw it out.

"Peaky & Spike with Night & Noon"

"Flashback (Peaky & Spike Go to Haight-Ashbury)" (page 124) also uses the setting-square option. The sashing is the same width as a unit in the five-patch block. *Peakies* are added around the interior setting squares. The overall effect did <u>not</u> become too complicated: the solid spaces between the blocks open up the design, and the setting-square stars connect the blocks enough to help hold the design together.

"Flashback (Peaky & Spike Go to Haight-Ashbury)"

Another example of setting square stars can be seen in the next drawing. The block is a five-patch that started out as nine-patch *Peaky & Spike* with *Wingy Things*. I added a row of units around it, turning it into a five-patch. When I set it with sashing the same width as the units in the block, I saw I could duplicate the original nine-patch at the setting square. *Wingy Things* had to be added to the corners to make it work. By using the same background fabric for block and sash, I made the stars appear to float (page 125).

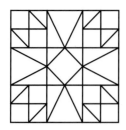

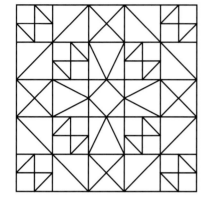

"Office Quilt"

I took the same idea one step further in "Peaky & Spike Go to Africa" (page 128). The original block was drawn on an uneven grid, giving us peakier *Peakies* and wingier *Wingy Things*. The original, undistorted nine-patch appears at the setting square. "St. Elsewhere" (page 121) and "Peaky & Spike Go to the Great Barrier Reef" (page 124) are further examples of original blocks with setting-square designs.

What I love about this whole concept is the great variety of styles and of quilts I can design. From "Ohio Star" (page 98), which has a comfortable, familiar feel, to "Peaky & Spike Go to the Great Barrier Reef" (page 124), which doesn't, the principle is the same. I have included some basic grids for setting variations (pages 80-83). The squares measure 1½" square, so you can place your own blocks into them.

"Peaky & Spike Go to Africa"

I give you these examples, quilts, and diagrams not just so you can copy them. I hope that, by studying what I have done, I am giving you a foot up to creating your own quilts. It is very important that you get your ideas down on paper. Sometimes I draw the quilt completely on graph paper; at other times I am able to take advantage of the copy machine and do more cutting and pasting than actual drawing. Recently, I have used the computer to draw, cut, and paste without pen, scissors, or glue. The method isn't important, but having a complete drawing of your quilt is. It is by looking at the black-and-white line drawing of a quilt that you can find the unexpected elements in the design. The drawing is also essential for developing a piecing plan, especially with the setting-strip options. It is from the diagram that you can make decisions about what needs to be sewn together first, what next, and so on. Will a one-way fabric affect the design? Do I need to work out a plan for fabric use, to be sure I have enough fabric to finish the piece? Can I eliminate some lines in the design, in order to simplify piecing? The diagram is my map: I keep it pinned up in front of me all the time I'm working on a quilt. Because I think of it as a map, I feel free to change course when necessary; but I can still keep an eye on my destination.

Setting layout: full width sashing

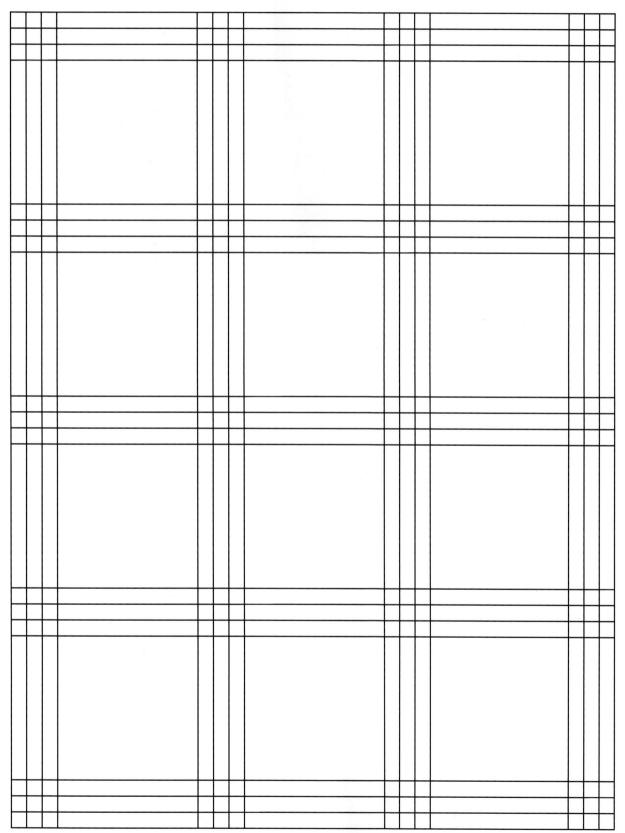

Checkerboard setting layout

Streak of Lightning setting layout

Offset square setting layout

COLOR AND FABRICS IN QUILTS

For me, color selection is the most aggravating, most exciting, most depressing, and most rewarding part of making a quilt. Color in the form of fabric makes all these quilt designs either sing or fall flat. The fabric color helps to create the new images from traditional designs.

A few words on classical color theory: I believe it. Wiser folks than I have devoted lifetimes to the study of color. I've read the books and taken a few classes, and I can proudly say that I know what a color wheel is and how it works. I can sit in the company of people who throw around words like *tint, tone, shade, hue, value, analogous,* and *complement* and understand what they are talking about. I don't think any time spent in the study of color is ever wasted. The problem comes when I try to apply all this theory to printed fabric. The rules must apply, because I believe they are just as basic and universal as simple tools are to any mechanical device. But, when I play with fabric, I can't think of any of these rules or theories.

I love fabric. I love buying it, refolding it, and stacking it neatly by color. I also love getting it out and finding more fabrics that go together. This is the most enjoyable part of making a quilt. When I'm playing with fabric combinations, I usually don't have a particular quilt in mind: I'm looking for an interesting combination of fabric. Sometimes this starts with a fantastic multicolored print. I then look for other fabric that brings out the colors in the first print. As I add to the pile, I look for a range of values from light to dark, and a variety of print texture from dainty calicoes and cabbage roses to tone-on-tone geometrics. The more individual fabrics I include, the less I have to worry about insufficient yardage. How do I know if a fabric belongs in the pile? Here's the key to my whole color theory. If I take it away, do I miss it? When I put it back, am I glad it is there? Sometimes the fabric screams at me, saying either "I belong in this quilt!" or "Put me back on the shelf!" Sometimes it just whispers. And there are times when it doesn't say anything at all. Though this may sound a little eccentric, I do believe this method puts our intuitive color sense to work. We all come to quiltmaking with our own color sensibilities. Though the decisions we make will often fall in line with traditional color theory, it is the quirkiness of our individual preferences that keeps quiltmaking from being an exact science.

My goal is always to use as many fabrics as possible. If one turquoise is good, three is better, and eight is better yet. As the pile grows, often I get a mental association with the fabrics. A lot of chintz florals remind me of English country gardens. There are general associations with color and fabric that we could all identify with: the seasons, the elements, a tropical rain forest, a Fourth of July parade. If I can take those assumptions and do something I've never seen before, all the better. Some color associations might be more personal—your grandma's living room is probably different from mine. The quilt "Cross Street Pasture" was so named because the fabric reminded me of day lilies against the plywood cows we have in our garden.

Design Board: I find it essential to lay out my work on a vertical surface before I sew anything together. Though my sewing room is small, I have kept one wall clear to use as a design wall. We first nailed firring strips to the wall and then nailed sound-deadening board to the firring strips. Sound-deadening board is like cheap bulletin-board material, available at building-supply stores. You want something that you can stick pins into. To hold the smaller cut pieces of fabric, cover the board with felt, flannel, or fleece. Felt is a good bargain, because it comes 72" wide in a variety of colors. With the board covered, you can lay up the smaller pieces without pins, and use pins to try out borders.

If a permanent installation isn't in the stars, you can create a temporary design surface by covering manageably small pieces of foam core on one side with felt. Link the covered rectangles with duct tape (the non-handywoman's best friend). Punch little holes in the back of the foam core to match up with nails on the wall. The whole outfit can be folded up and slipped under the bed when not in use.

You've probably noticed that I haven't mentioned what quilt design goes with which pile of fabrics. Often that is dictated by how big the pile is. If I am planning to make a queen-size quilt, I avoid those fabric piles with fat quarters and half-yard pieces, looking instead for a fabric grouping that contains bigger pieces or might be easier to expand. I do give yardages for all the quilts in the back section of the book, but you need to know that these were all figured out by hindsight. I've never sat down and figured all my yardages before starting a quilt. That would assume that everything was going to work out exactly as I had planned. It never does!

When I'm ready to start applying fabric to quilt design, I first lay all of the fabric out in front of me. Then I look for colored pencils that match the fabrics as closely as possible. Keep in mind that one colored pencil can color light, medium, and dark. But it will come as no news to most of you that colored pencils do not reproduce all the richness and subtlety of printed fabric—not unless you buy fabric to match your colored pencils. But I match pencils and fabric anyway.

Next, I look at the design and try to figure out what parts I want to be prominent. The most important thing to do now is just make some kind of decision to put some fabric somewhere. When I've colored it in, I separate that fabric from the pile and lay it in front of me. I might be influenced by trying to put the large-scale prints in areas where the shapes are large. Each quilt is different, and each decision relies on factors that are hard to write about in general. But the method works every time I've used it. So I continue coloring and laying out the fabric, trying to duplicate as much as possible the proportions and relation-ships I will use in the actual quilt. When I look at the colored drawing, I see the fabric, not the pencils. I can see if I will need more blues or reds and what fabrics in the pile just don't fit into this quilt. Then I can go back to my regular fabric storage area and look for additions. Again the "miss it" theory comes in handy: if I'm not sure whether a fabric belongs, I take it out to see if I miss it. This process continues until I don't know what to do next, or all the fabric decisions have been made.

Does all this playing around with color and fabric guarantee that your quilt is going to turn out great? Can you just cut those pieces and sew? I wish I could say yes. I've learned that with each quilt there comes a point where you can't make color decisions ahead of time. I've struggled, trying to determine whether the secondary stars should be blue or turquoise, or what background is best. Each quilt has a different stumbling block. I no longer worry when I get to those points. If I'm fairly happy with the choices up to there, I figure the solution will come to me when I get the rest cut out and put up on a design board. However much pre-planning, coloring, arranging, or rationalizing we do, we cannot escape another of the fabric truths.

Nothing looks more like the fabric cut to the size it is going to be, next to what it is going to be next to, better than the fabric cut to the size it is going to be, next to what it is going to be next to. That sounds confusing, I know, but no amount of intellectualizing can compete with looking at the fabric laid out like the quilt. The holes can be filled in, because now, with more pieces cut and the quilt taking shape on

Other ideas that work in a pinch:

1. The fleece back of a vinyl tablecloth is not great to pin into, but it will hold small pieces.

2. Seam lengths of fleece flat together. Sew a rod pocket across the top and insert a curtain rod. Hang it from small nails placed near the ceiling. No one will ever notice them when the fleece is taken down. To work well, the fleece should hang close to the wall; air movement will send the pieces flying.

the wall, we have more information to work with.

Look at your piece as it develops. If there is one fabric that sticks out when you hoped it would blend, or if an area you colored in to show up prominently doesn't, change it. That sounds obvious, but so often we leave something in just because we have cut the piece. This is false economy. You still have months and years to live with the choices you make now.

If the piece doesn't look as I had planned, there is usually one of two problems. Either an area I had planned to read as one flowing color looks chopped up or spotty, or an area I planned as prominent can't be distinguished from its background. In either case, the solution usually lies in adjusting the value or contrast. When I want a range of blues to read as one, none of them can be wildly lighter or darker than its companions. This doesn't mean they should be all the exact same value—that's boring. I use a range of fabrics to break up an area and make it visually more interesting. On the other hand, if an area that I wanted to see floating above its background is sinking into it, I need to widen the contrast between them by either darkening or lightening one or them.

I think of value as numbers on fabrics. If the lightest fabric is #1 and the darkest fabric is #10, the contrast between them is strong because the values are farthest apart. Fabrics in the 7-8-9 range will blend because they are too near each other in value.

Another way to separate areas, besides using strong contrast, is to change from warm to cool fabric. In "Hearts of Space," the red and green fabrics are very close in value. When I photographed them in black and white, I couldn't distinguish the hearts from the spaces. The design works because of the strong line created between red (warm) and green (cool). Hot colors are those that remind of us of sun or fire—red, orange, yellow, peach, rust, pink. Cool colors remind us of air and water—blue, green teal, turquoise, forest. The strongest line can be created by strong value differences and a change of temperature.

I use numbers in another stage of matching quilt and fabric. I think you have to be a "counter" to appreciate this, someone who counts the railroad cars at a crossing because they are there. When I have an area to fill with blue and have five blues to do it with, I give each blue a number. Then I make some sort of number pattern on the diagram in the area that will be blue. (See page 87.) If I weren't a "counter," this would strike me as foolishness. But it is wonderful way to aid the decision-making process. I am often surprised by the resulting transparencies when those fabrics range from blue to turquoise or even dark beige to light beige.

If you can make enough sense out of this color discussion to give it a try, I think you'll be amazed at how well it works. We wouldn't be attracted to making quilts if we did not love fabric and color. Most quiltmakers I know seem to have mastered buying fabrics. Yet we freeze when it's time to put them together. If we stop waiting for a color expert to come into our studios and tell us what to do, we will find great depths of color understanding in ourselves. You'd be surprised whom I am willing to consider a color expert when I'm desperate: a fifteen-year-old who could hardly care and a husband who probably cares less. They humor me and at times give helpful suggestions. But the real decisions and total understanding of the project are within us, and the process starts with the first decision.

ADDITIONAL THOUGHTS
ABOUT COLOR

1. You can put almost any fabrics together in a quilt if you can find a bridge or connector—that fabric that makes the transition seem normal and natural.

2. The bigger the variety of fabrics you have in the quilt, the easier it is to add fabrics. For example, if you have fifteen reds from china red to cherry, you can easily add five more reds, no matter how orange or blue or light or dark those reds are. If you have only two reds, a third one must be chosen with more care.

3. Good decisions get better and bad ones get worse, but you have to make one to start the process. Often when I have changed something in a quilt for the third or fourth time, I'm so confused I don't know if my fifth choice is good or bad. I leave the room, fill the dishwasher, get the mail in, come back and look. If it looks better to me each time I look, then I must be on the right track. A bad choice will look worse every time I walk in the room. The orange stars in "Sea of Stars" (page 127) were my eighth choice. By the time I put the orange in, I was just grateful it didn't make me sick. But it started to grow on me, and soon I wondered what had taken me so long to choose.

4. Sometimes putting colors and fabrics together is just plain hard. I now take this for granted and enjoy the challenge. Some people jump out of airplanes for excitement; I put purple and peach in the same quilt. If I wanted to do something easy, I'd make refrigerator magnets out of colored foam and buggy eyes. The challenge is what keeps so many of us quiltmaking after years of experience with other needlework forms.

5. Act with conviction. I have seen some of the most outrageous fabrics and colors put in the same quilt. It worked because the quiltmaker didn't back down.

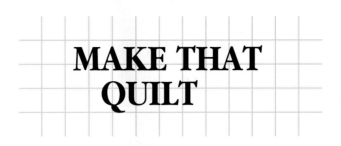

MAKE THAT QUILT

Designing quilt blocks and quilts is so much fun that it could be an end in itself—but then there would be no reason to collect fabric! At some point, we have to say to ourselves, "It's time to make a quilt."

TEMPLATES

Before we can start cutting fabric, we have to figure out how we are going to put the quilt together. As quiltmakers of the 1990's, we have more options open to us than quiltmakers of the 1890's. With the introduction of the rotary cutter, new quiltmaking techniques have been developed. But most of what I do does not lend itself to standard quick-piecing techniques. After the quilt is finished, I can look back and see where I could have cut strips for easy four-patches or sheeted half-square triangles. The problem is that I usually don't know which fabric is going to end up in the quilt. (You'll understand that better if you have read the section on color and fabric.) I find it much easier, and definitely more accurate, to work with templates. (Don't you love how people who write books are always sure their way is the best?) If you are a new quilter, cutting your pieces from templates is a straight-forward, time-tested, and thoroughly wonderful way to make quilts. If you are an experienced rotary-cutting quiltmaker, humor me and try it.

Before you can actually make the templates for the quilt you have designed, you need to analyze your design to see what blocks are in it. Next, look at the blocks and identify the basic components. From the basic components you can see what templates you will need. I'll use "Amanda's Quilt" (page 97) as an example of the process I'd follow with any of the quilt designs. "Amanda's Quilt" is made up of two different blocks: Ohio Star and *Peaky & Spike with Corners*.

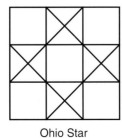

Ohio Star

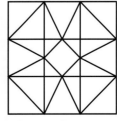

Peaky & Spike with Corners

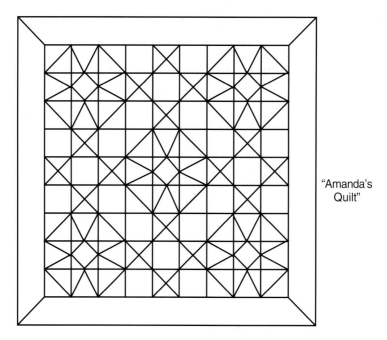

"Amanda's Quilt"

Now is a good time to think about size. When making a nine-patch, I don't want to start with some weird, difficult-to-divide block size like 10". But, if we make each unit 4", the block will measure 12" and the quilt 36" before borders. With 3" finished units, the block is 9" and the quilt 27". For this quilt I am going to work with 4" units.

I look to each block in order to identify first the basic components, then the individual shapes or templates I will need. For the Ohio Star we need a 4" *Square* and a 4" *Trickies (Quarter-Square Triangles)*, or two templates.

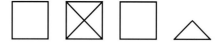

The basic components for the other block are the *Half-Square Triangle, Peaky & Spike,* and the *Center Diamond.* Therefore this will require five templates. You should analyze your design in the same way.

In order to make sturdy templates you need: accurate ¼" graph paper, a sharp pencil, a sturdy transparent ruler with a ¼" line parallel to the edge, rubber cement, template plastic, and scissors (<u>not</u> your best fabric-cutting ones). To make templates:

1. Draw the exact size and shape of your pattern on graph paper. We have the exact measurements of at least two sides, or some internal measurements. Go from what you know. The 4" *Square* has four 4" sides—easy. The 4" *Half-Square Triangle* has two 4" sides and a square corner, and the 4" *Trickies* has one 4" side. The 4" *Center Diamond* can't be drawn from the length of its sides, but we know that it has to measure 4" from point to opposite point. The same is true of the *Trickies*. We know the long side must measure 4" and to the point 2". Use those measurements to set the points and connect. *Peaky & Spike* are easy to do. We know *Spike* must measure 4" on its base and 4" from the middle of that base to the point. I don't know what any of the angles are, but I know that it will finish into the 4" component. *Peaky* measures 2" on one side with a square corner and a 4" side.

2. In order to avoid future panic, label the template patterns right now by their measurements. When I started making quilts, I was told to make templates for a block, identify them by the block they were used in, and store those templates together in an envelope. I had envelopes full of 4" half-square triangles. Because these templates are so interchangeable, it is more efficient to make one really good set and pull out the appropriate pieces as you need them. You may want to spend a night making a complete set for all the basic components as 4", 3", and 2" finished squares. Label them accurately. Then, when you start a project that uses any of the basic components, you can just sort out the templates you are going to use.

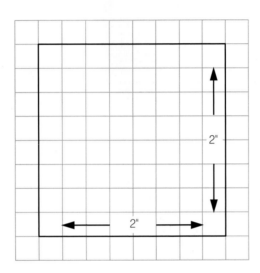

3. Add ¼" seam allowance to all sides of each template. Use the graph-paper lines on the straight sides, and the ¼" line on the ruler for the diagonals. Use a felt-tip marker or very sharp pencil to add this line, so the line is directly against the ruler. If the pencil is dull, you'll see "gaposis" between ruler and line; then the template won't be the right size, and your quilt will be a mess.

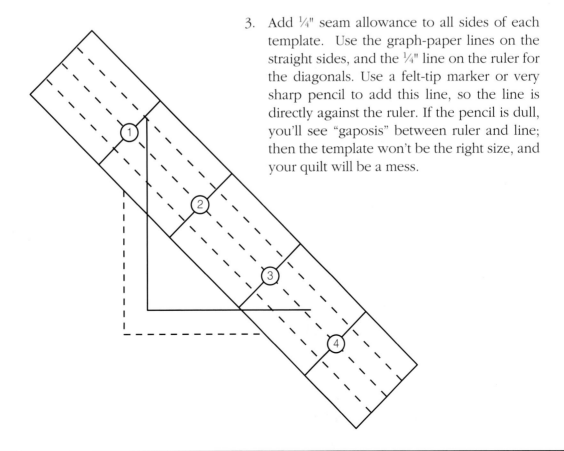

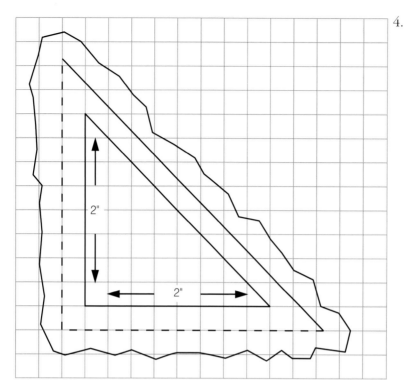

4. Cut templates apart—but not on the line yet, just loosely outside the seam allowance line.

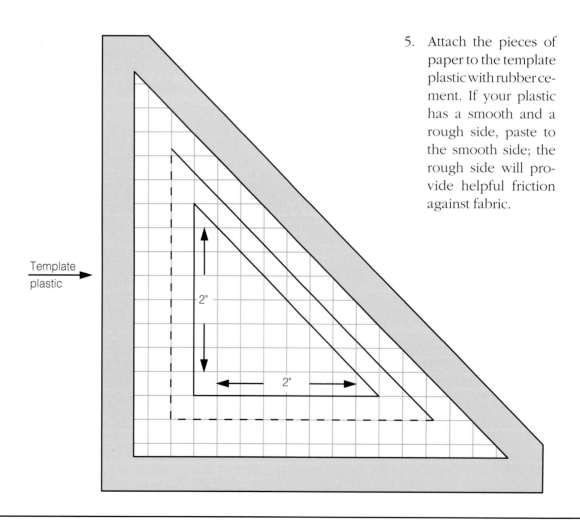

Template plastic

5. Attach the pieces of paper to the template plastic with rubber cement. If your plastic has a smooth and a rough side, paste to the smooth side; the rough side will provide helpful friction against fabric.

6. Now cut template paper and plastic at the same time. You do <u>not</u> want to include the <u>thickness</u> of the ruler lines: there should be no black line remaining on the template!

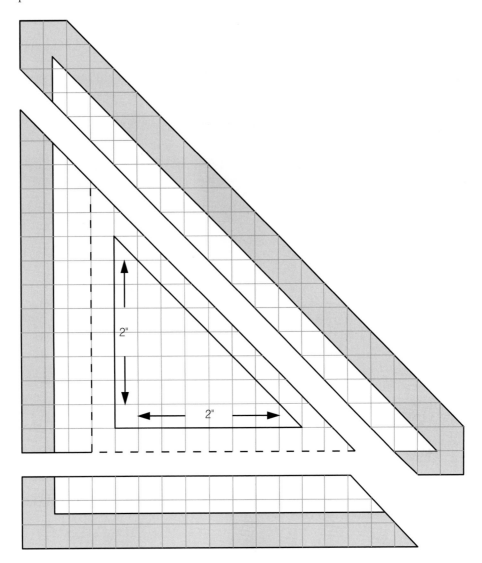

Accuracy: The time spent making accurate templates will more than pay off when your quilt goes together with a hitch. <u>Do not use templates that have been copied on a regular copy machine.</u> There always seems to be a little distortion as the image passes over the drum. The templates on the fold-out in this book have been printed and are perfect.

We have been using 4" finished units for our examples. Similar templates can be made for 3" finished or 2" finished units. Instead of 4" and 2" as the key numbers, use 3" and 1½", or 2" and 1". All of the lines in each component either start in a corner and end in a corner, start in the middle and end in the middle, or start in a corner and end in the middle. Look at the shape of the component and you will be able to figure out the significant measurements. Knowing how to look at a design and analyze it for templates has given me a freedom that I wouldn't trade for anything. When you can make your own templates, you are no longer at the mercy of someone else's design, scale or size limitations, or inaccurate printing.

Before we talk about where the grainline should go, maybe this is the time to explain what grain is. When fabric is woven, warp threads are run through the loom. These threads are turned into fabric when woof threads are woven over and under the warp. The fabric has two straight grains. The <u>lengthwise</u> grain runs with the warp, parallel to the edges of the fabric, and it has almost no give at all. <u>Crosswise</u> grain is perpendicular to the edge of the fabric, running from selvage to selvage, and it has a little give. Both of these are considered straight grains. When we cross these grains at an angle, we create a bias. True <u>bias</u> is at a 45° angle to the edge and is the stretchiest part of the fabric. All other angles are some kind of bias and are fairly stretchy. We want to avoid having the outside of our quilts on the bias: they will handle better, and the quilt will hang better, if most of the pieces are cut along the grain. (I find it easier to sew similar biases together than trying to sew a bias to a straight grainline.)

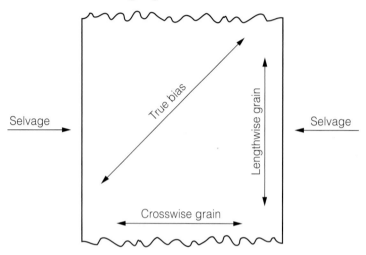

Now that I have stated a rule that governs most of my quiltmaking, I freely admit to you that I break that rule whenever I need to. If a fabric has some special element that I want to capture on the quilt, I ignore grainlines and do what needs to be done. Stripes or border prints can be cut to create some interesting and unusual patterns when sewn together, if you are willing to ignore grainline and cut to fit the spot. It is usually well worth the trouble. (Designing hint for working with stripe fabric: Take the fabric to the copy machine. It is much cheaper to make mistakes with the paper in trying out different effects. You'll be surprised at how well fabric copies.)

YARDAGE

In my own quiltmaking, I've never been very interested in figuring yardage before I start a project, although there are times during a project when I've run out of fabric and wish I had calculated beforehand. My solution is to keep a good supply of fabric on hand but view a shortage as an opportunity to add variety. (It's my version of "living on the edge.") Every quilt that has required an additional fabric choice is better for the substitution. The shortfalls have encouraged me to vary backgrounds, alternate star-point colors, or get on the phone and beg friends for a little piece of fabric we bought at the same time. If you haven't been collecting fabric for twenty years (I started collecting before I started quilting) and don't like to live that courageously, you will find the yardage charts on the inside back cover flap helpful.

When you have made your fabric choices, you can write your own quilt recipe. For example, in "Amanda's Quilt" I needed four 4" right triangles of background for the *Peaky* Star block, and four 4" squares and four 4" *Trickies* for the Ohio Star block. Multiply those numbers by the number of blocks in the quilt to get totals. Then refer to the yardage chart for a very generous yardage estimate.

Fabric	Size	Shape	# in block		blocks in quilt	Total
Tulip	4"	square	4	x	4	= 16
	4"	*Trickies*	4	x	4	= 16
	4"	right triangles	4	x	5	= 20

From a quarter-yard I can cut sixteen 4" squares or sixteen 4" right triangles. I can cut thirty-six 4" *Trickies* from a quarter-yard, though I need only sixteen. So, three-quarters of a yard of fabric will be enough to cut all the pieces I need: the four extra 4" right triangles can come out of the excess estimate for the *Trickies*.

The figures are for regular fabric with all-over prints, cut on grain. Using stripes or isolating elements in a fabric really eats up the yardage. Buy lots and hope for the best. When we use fabric in interesting ways, one of the repercussions is the difficulty of estimating yardage. I have used up a yard of fabric capturing the orange roses on a piece of fabric that was mostly purple. This I call "Swiss-cheese cutting," because that's what the fabric looks like when you are done.

I hesitate in bringing up this next point, because I feel I'm encouraging obsessive-compulsive behavior in quiltmakers. There are some sneaky fabrics on the market that appear to be all-over prints. We might pick them up to use for background or points in a star. On closer examination, we discover that what we have is definitely a one-way print—bubbles that go up, tulips with all the stems down. A variation of this kind of print is one where the tulip stems go both up and down, and we are essentially dealing with a stripe fabric. In either case, we might as well be working with corduroy. If we cut this fabric just willy-nilly, the visual effect could be just as distracting as badly cut corduroy. What are the choices? The most obvious is not to use that fabric. Look for another that you don't have to worry about. Another choice is to cut it any way you want and ignore the fabric pattern flipping all over the quilt. There are free-spirit quiltmakers who would consider that perfectly appropriate behavior. Ah, to be so free....

Some of us are in the other group: "obsessive-compulsives in training" may be the kindest way to describe us. It would drive us crazy to have all the fleur-de-lis pointing anywhere but up. Should this attitude be encouraged? I yam what I yam! I love the feeling I get when bullying those tulips into their proper place; I think this is a "control issue." Some people race cars or climb mountains; I make bubbles bubble in one direction only. It's not that hard to do, with a little pre-planning. Knowledge is power; if you know how to do it, you can decide whether it is necessary or not. You must first decide what you want the fabric to do. Should the design all go up and down? Would it be more effective radiating from the center? Again I think it is easier to work with paper. Make a drawing of what you want to achieve and monitor where the lengthwise grain is. Cut accordingly. Here are a few examples of blocks, with possible choices and how you can get them by proper cutting.

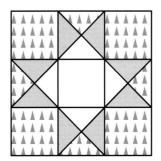

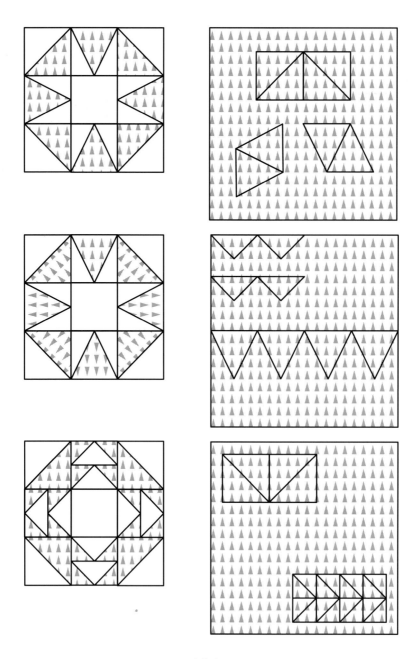

CUTTING

There is no "one and only" way to approach cutting the pieces for a quilt. When auditioning a fabric for the quilt, you will want to cut just enough pieces for a few blocks—enough to see if you like it. When the decisions have been made, you may want to employ methods more appropriate to cutting many pieces quickly.

This brings us to the question of whether "to rotary cut or not to rotary cut." Sometimes we approach adopting a method as if we were making a religious decision: if we use the rotary cutter, we must <u>always</u> use the rotary cutter. I think it makes more sense to use the method most appropriate and comfortable for the moment and project. It is silly to rotary cut when I need only four 2" triangles; it is easier for me just to trace around the template and cut with scissors. It is probably equally silly to cut out two hundred 2" squares with scissors when I own a rotary cutter. I love to cut my quilt pieces with scissors, efficient or not, because I love my chair, the proximity to the ironing board, and the unobstructed view of the television. Keep this advice in mind as you read my instructions; try all the methods, and choose the appropriate one for your situation and your mind-set.

Amanda's Quilt
42" x 42"
hand quilted
Collection of Amanda Punzel

Storm at Sea
90" x 76"
hand quilted
Collection of
Bobbie Rottier

Peaky & Spike Go to Australia
45" x 45"
hand quilted

Ohio Star
60" x 47"
hand quilted

Peaky & Spike Go to
the Grand Caymans
42" x 42"
hand quilted

Ambrosia
96" x 75"
hand quilted

Eye of the Storm
87" x 60"
hand quilted
Collection of Sievers School of Fiber Arts

Sally's Stars
64" x 42"
hand quilted

Christmas Rose
48" x 48"
unquilted top

Christmas Rose
48" x 48"
unquilted top

Storm at Sea with Churn Dash
44" x 44"
machine quilted by Dalene Young Thomas

Cheap Trick
76" x 76"
unquilted top

Bahamian Blossoms
50" x 50"
unquilted top

Butter Churn
43" x 43"
hand quilted
Collection of Sara Miller

Cross Street Pasture
80" x 58"
hand quilted

Sort out the templates you need for your project. Then prepare your fabric. It is a good idea to re-fold the fabric so right sides are together, because it is easier to see pencil marks on the wrong side of some fabrics and, if you make a mistake, the front of the fabric isn't marked up. Work with fabric doubled, because the two layers seem to stabilize each other, especially when they are freshly pressed. Trace around the template with a pencil. Be sure the line is fine and is right against the edge of the template. Position the template to share a line with another piece whenever possible, saving both cutting and fabric (but avoid using the selvage).

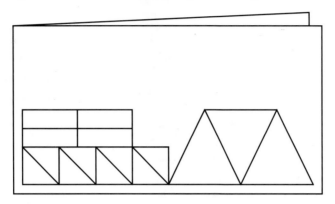

Working with sharp fabric-only scissors, cut carefully on the lines. For visually complicated quilts, I put all the pieces on the design board, because I might have to make changes, and I need to see the piece in its entirety. For a simpler, identical-block repeat, I leave one or two blocks on the board as inspiration. The rest of the cut pieces I stack together by unit in a gift box. (I don't buy a pair of socks at Marshall Field's without asking for a box.)

Modified Rotary-Scissors Cutting

There are situations when it is appropriate to use both rotary cutter and scissors with templates. You need a 6" x 24" clear ruler and removable sticky notes. We want to cut a strip of fabric exactly as wide as the template is high. We could measure the template, but I think it is simpler to mark the ruler by standing both ruler and template on edge on the table. Toward each end of the ruler, place a sticky note just off the tip of the template. Use notes as your guide to cutting the strips of fabric.

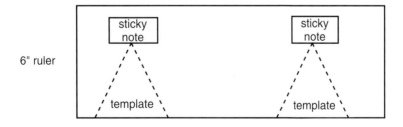

Now use the template to make the other cuts. I would mark and cut with scissors, but you may prefer to make cuts with a rotary cutter.

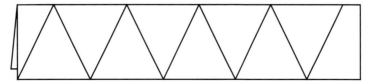

I would use the rotary cutter only to cut squares or rectangles. Using templates keeps me from getting sloppy. How well your pieces are cut is directly responsible for how well they will sew together. I would rather fuss a little with the cutting than have to sew and rip, sew and rip, sew and rip, sew and rip.

MACHINE SEWING

How are you going to put your quilt together? As quilters, we have the option of sewing by hand or machine. When I started making quilts fifteen years ago, I had heard that it wasn't a quilt if it wasn't sewn by hand. I carried that guilty burden, but sewed my quilts on the sewing machine anyway. People like to defend their method with a fervor that sometimes borders on fanaticism: they assure you that the only way to create an adequate product is to do it _their_ way. I, however, see method as a means to an end—and that means usually is chosen because it most conveniently fits our lifestyle. When I questioned hand piecers, I found what they really liked about sewing by hand was where they could sew: in an easy chair watching TV, in the car, on the train to work, at their child's hockey or baseball game. I hand quilt in my easy chair, but I can't even look in my purse while riding in a car without feeling woozy, and I don't have a child on a sports team (she dances instead). I love my sewing machine and love to feed fabric through it. It I didn't make quilts, I would find something to sew. I like my sewing space: first floor, close to the bathroom, within earshot of the kitchen timer. I won't give instructions for hand piecing because I would feel like a hypocrite, but you certainly could piece your quilts by hand.

Set-Up and Supplies

Sewing Machine: Contrary to the sales pitches, you do _not_ need a state-of-the-art sewing machine. Any machine with a good straight stitch will make beautiful patchwork. For thirteen years I made every quilt (and most of my clothing) on a Singer 201® machine that only goes forward and backward and was last made in 1955. Its little sister, the Singer 221 Featherweight®, is well known as a good machine to piece with. I now have a Pfaff Creative 1475 CD® that does everything from sewing a beautiful stitch to making signed labels for my quilts. And there are a number of other excellent machines that I don't happen to own.

What _is_ important is whether your machine sews a good lock stitch. You can aid that function by getting out the instruction book to locate the cleaning and oiling points. Then CLEAN and OIL. Change the needle even when it is not broken. The Schmetz[tm] 80/12 needles are a good size for most cotton fabrics. A little loving care can do wonders for any sewing machine.

If you are using a zigzag machine, check whether you can change the throat plate. The throat plate for zigzagging has a large opening under the needle. Temperamental machines like to suck the fabric points down that hole. If you can use the straight stitch throat plate instead, that problem is solved. Just don't switch to a zigzag stitch without changing back to the zigzag plate.

The Foot: I feel strongly that the foot on your sewing machine should be open to the needle. With the open toe, you can follow the matching points with your eyes all the way to the needle. As the patchwork grows from units to blocks, this becomes ever more important.

Unlike many piecers I know, I'm not the least bit interested in whether my presser foot measures ¼" from the needle to the edge. I don't use the edge of the foot as my sewing guide: by the time you know whether or not your seam allowance is ¼", it's too late. I like to have the ¼" seam allowance marked on the sewing machine well in front of the needle, so pieces can be lined up and fed through. One of the best ways to be sure that you are taking away the same seam allowance that you have added to the template is to put the template itself under the presser foot. Position the template so that, when the needle is lowered, it hits the seam line. After checking to see if the right edge of template is perpendicular to the front edge of the sewing machine, lay a piece of tape or a sticky note along that edge. In this way you can be sure the seam allowance you take is the same one you added. If you have made accurate templates, cut fabric the same size as your templates, and sewn with the same seam allowance you added, your piecing will be perfect.

Thread: Try to find a color that matches, or at least blends, for sewing patchwork. What you don't want to see are little white spots of thread ("peekers") at the seams. I prefer 100% cotton thread. My favorite is Star® thread. The long staple polyester threads from Switzerland and Germany will do a good job also. If you see thread in a basket that reads "10 spools for $1," remember that you get what you pay for—or less. You will pay double in time lost if you work with crummy materials.

Thread Clippers: Get some. A pair of thread snips or clippers will prolong the life of your good scissors for years. If you don't have clippers yet, use any scissors except your good ones to clip threads.

Get ready, get set...: Make the area around your sewing machine as safe and efficient as possible. Clear a path to your design board. Have your iron and ironing board handy. Wind five or six bobbins, so you can keep sewing. Take a good look at your design board. If there is something up there that is irritating you now, change it; otherwise, it will only get worse. Set your stitch length to about 15 stitches per inch or 2.0 on European machines, and you're ready to go.

Sew: In general, what you want to do now is sew the pieces into the basic components or units you used in the design process. Then you can assemble the small squares into larger and larger sections, until the quilt is all together. Each quilt has its own piecing strategy. It is wise to have an overall plan in your head before you start.

I've learned from (unpleasant) experience that it is wisest never to take more off the board than you can put back in the right place. Look at the quilt to find identical units: same lines, same fabrics. Pull them off, sew them together, and put them back. If you have trouble absorbing this idea, think of the story one of my students told. Her family runs a nursing home. They didn't think they had to tell a new employee not to pick up all the false teeth at once. So she did. It made sense as she was picking them up; getting them back in the right place was another story. The rule holds for fabric as well as for teeth. Start slowly. As the quilt grows, you will be able to handle more.

If we have a general idea of where we are going, let's now get specific about how to sew each of the units together. The basic components break down into different families for construction. Each family has its own rules that govern how the pieces will sew together accurately. I think it is a good idea to do a few trial runs when working with new shapes. Either cut pieces from crummy fabric or use the leftover replaced-by-a-better-fabric pieces. Practice sewing the units together; measure to be sure they are the exact finished size you had planned plus seam allowance (4½", 3½", 2½"). You can catch errors in seam allowance now and not have to rip later.

Pressing: Whenever possible, press the seams to <u>one</u> side (not open) and toward the darker fabric. Press from the right side: the seams will be flatter. It is important to press after each sewing operation. It is a subtle step but, as you press, try to move with the grain of the fabric; that way you won't distort the bias edge.

Identical shapes: The easiest units to sew together are those constructed of identical shapes. There is no question of how to line them up, because they match perfectly. Identical units can then be sewn to more identical units: two 2" triangles when sewn become a 2" square. We can sew two 2" triangles and a square together into a 2" x 4" rectangle.

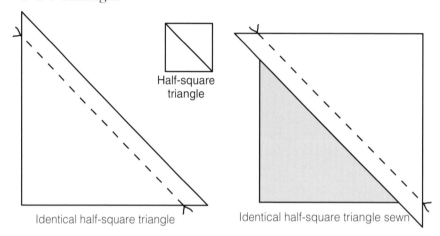

Half-square triangle

Identical half-square triangle   Identical half-square triangle sewn

Trickies (Quarter-Square Triangles): Both sets are pressed toward the darker fabric. When you flip them around for sewing, you will have opposing seams. You won't even need a pin to match them up: they will automatically fit together.

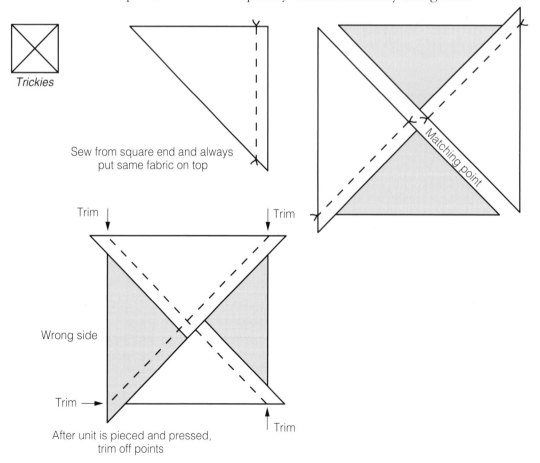

Trickies

Sew from square end and always put same fabric on top

Matching Point

Trim   Trim

Wrong side

Trim

Trim

After unit is pieced and pressed, trim off points

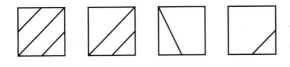

Not identical but no crossovers: When you are joining two pieces and you want a straight edge, line up the pieces so the little "ears" hang out evenly. Start and stop stitching in the crevices.

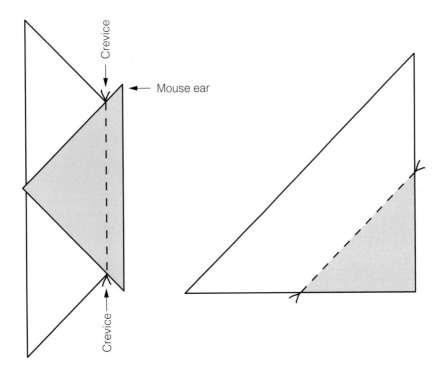

Two passes: The next group that operates under the same rules still has 45° angles. The pieces cross over each other, making one or more interior points. The rules change a little at the points. We'll use the *Center Diamond* as the first example.

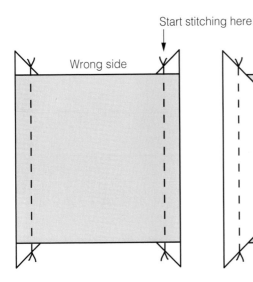
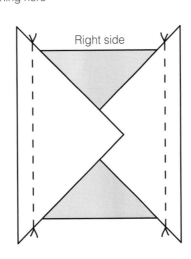

a. Line up the triangles on opposite sides of the square; "mouse ears" should hang out evenly. Notice when you take the ¼" seam that it does not start at the crevice. I wanted it to, but it's not right. You should see a few stitches on the triangle before you hit the square.

b. Press the seams away from the center.
c. Attach the other two triangles. Again the mouse ears will hang out evenly. This time sew from crevice to crevice. You know you've done it right when the edges are straight and the points are ¼" from the edge. Trim away the ears. When possible, press away from the square. Being able to see the "crossroads" is important when assembling units into blocks: they are the guideposts to the point on the right side.

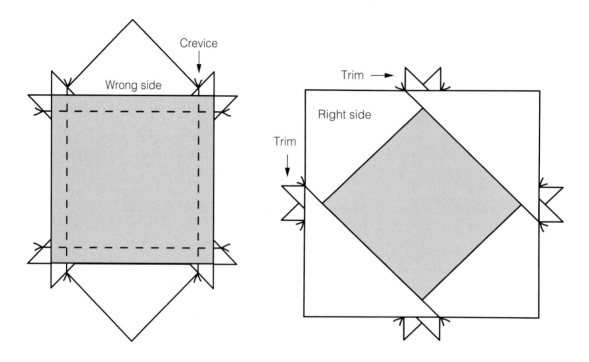

Another variation of two-pass piecing is the *Little House* unit. On one side, we want it to line up straight. In the middle, we have a crossover point. Line up the triangle so it meets the straight side with a ¼" crevice. The triangle will extend out further. You'll be stitching on the triangle after you've left the *Little House* shape. Then line up the second triangle so mouse ears hang out evenly and sew from crevice to crevice. Your finished *Little House* should look this. Trim points off even with edges.

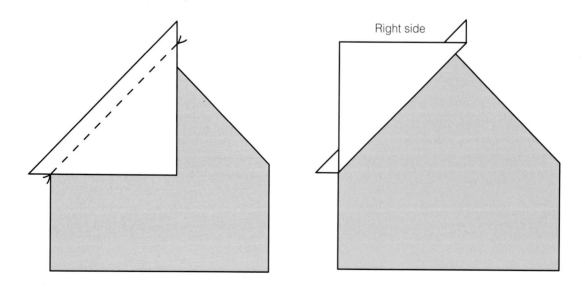

110

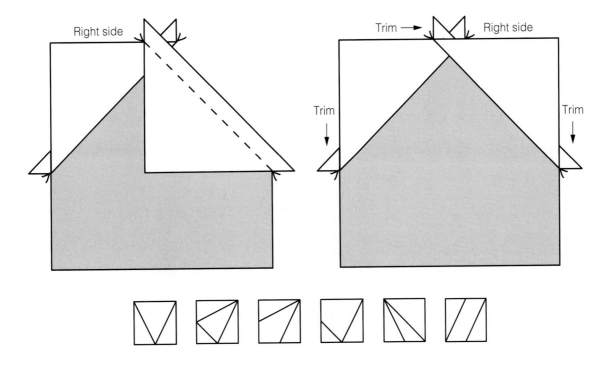

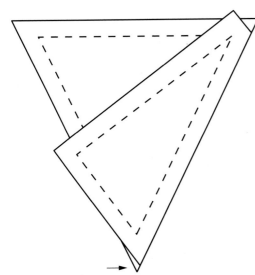

Weird angles: Now we come to the weird ones. I couldn't find any rules that applied, so for years I sewed them and just hoped for the best. I could have solved the problem by drawing in the seam line and pinning from point to point, duplicating the traditional hand piecing technique. Another alternative was to punch holes at the seam-line corners. Even when using an ⅛" paper punch, I found the holes too big and the results were only slightly better than the "happy accident" method. What I really needed was some guideline on how to line up the two pieces. The solution is to go directly to the templates. Hold them up to the light and match the seam lines. Tape them together. Look at this to see what is happening at each end of the seam.

Pick up the fabric and make it look like the templates.

Using *Peaky & Spike* as an example, sew from the upper right to the center.

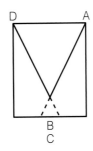

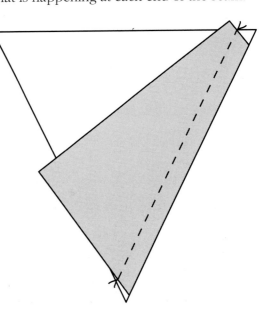

To sew the second *Peaky* on, lay it on top of the first *Peaky. Spike* is taller behind the twin peaks.

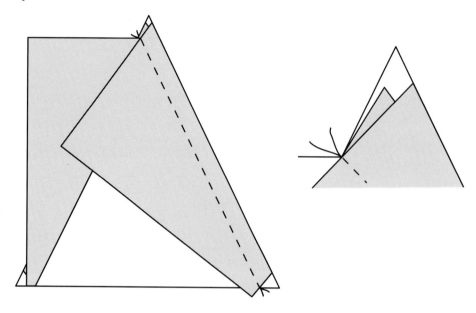

Here is what *Peaky & Spike* should look like finished.

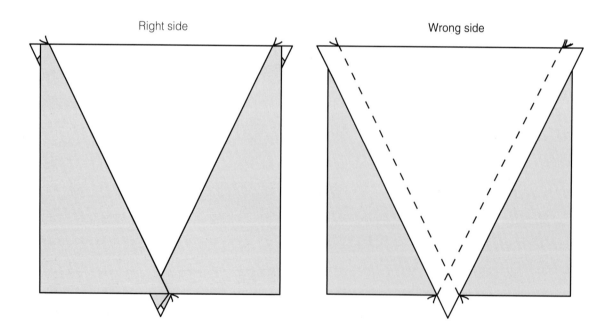

Right side

Wrong side

Ice Cream Cones: Here's another odd angle to deal with. Make a mock-up with templates to get your bearings. Note that you start sewing at the crevice. Press away from the cone. Sew the second *Peaky* onto the cone. Start at the end opposite from the point in the crevice.

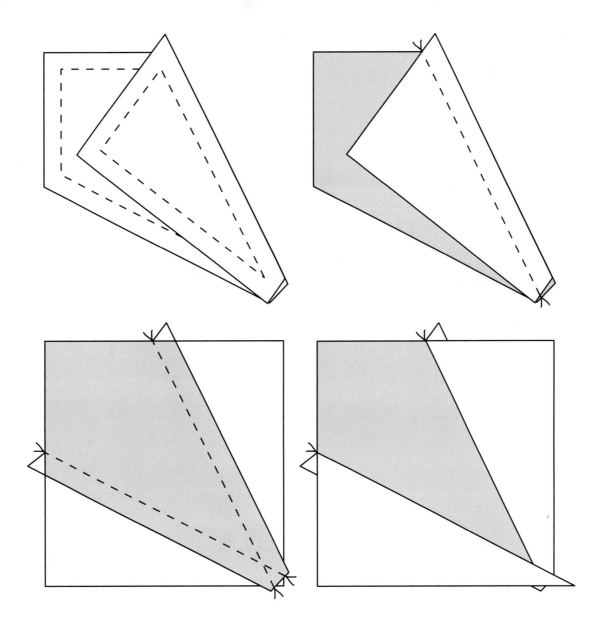

When all of the units are sewn together, pressed, and the mouse ears have been trimmed off, you are ready to assemble the quilt. Each quilt presents its own logical path. Often we follow the traditional route, assembling units into blocks and then sewing block to block or blocks to sashings. But there are times when you may assemble rows of units. The Card Trick group (pages 36 and 37) grows from the center out, with rows of units added around the center block or rectangle. The small lily quilts (pages 34 and 35) are put together as units, each of which contains four component pieces—the lilies themselves, the center, and the corners—then sewn together as a giant nine-patch. Make a plan and follow it. Whatever path you choose, continue to press consistently and, whenever possible, oppose the seams as we did in sewing units together. Consistent pressing will give you a flat top and make it easier to quilt. The best advice I can give you is to keep looking at the piece, checking to see that nothing is turned around. Better to catch those mistakes early, instead of after the borders are on! (That slip-up can make me cranky for days.)

Helpful Hint

There is a very low-tech method for matching points perfectly. The problem arises when you have two points that have to match but you can see only the side facing you as you put it through the sewing machine.

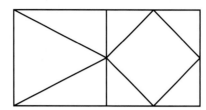

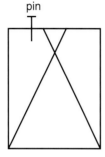

To get that perfect match, line up the units at the corners. Now peel back the seam allowances to reveal the points that need to match. With fingertips and eyeballs, match these points perfectly. Hold tightly to this spot until you wriggle a pin in just to the left of the crossroads.

Then sew the units together with a ¼" seam allowance, but aim to stitch across the crossroads even when the seam allowance may vary slightly.

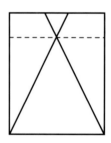

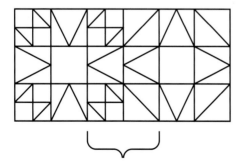

When you sew rows of units together, you may find that important crossroads fall on both sides of the rows.

You will be able to see those crossroads only on the top as you feed the fabric through the sewing machine. To solve the problem, sew partial seams. Line up and pin the units together, then sew a partial seam which intersects the visible crossroads.

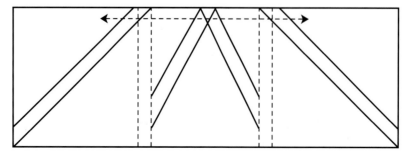

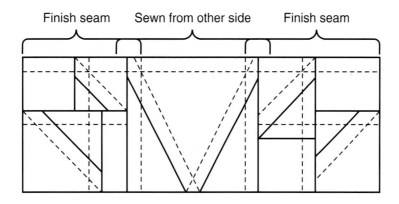

Finish seam   Sewn from other side   Finish seam

Then flip the rows over and finish the seam, intersecting the crossroads that now appear. Overlap the partial seams by at least 2 stitches. I've given you one example of this but it may come up in a number of different ways. The essential message here is to first use your eyes and fingertips to make your matches. Secondly if you can't see the match, consider sewing on both sides of the seam.

SETTING STRIPS

You may have chosen to use sashings in setting strips in your design. Whether the design is plain sashing or embellished with piecing around the setting square, the general method of construction is the same. Look at your drawing to establish a piecing plan.

My personal preference is to use the setting square in even the simplest setting. Though the setting strip with no square is visually the simplest, the assembly can be a little tricky. First of all, if we want to avoid seams in the setting strips, we need to have enough fabric to cut with the lengthwise grain. If the fabric is at all directional, the strips will be running up and down and crosswise and be annoying to look at. With the setting square option, no strip needs to be cut longer than the length of the blocks. We can cut all the strips on the crosswise grain, or cut both lengthwise and crossgrain strips and place them accordingly.

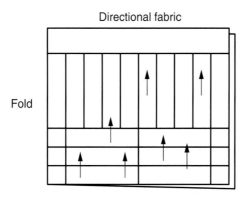

Directional fabric

Fold

We discussed grain in relation to cutting pieces for quilt blocks. It is again an issue with setting squares. Every book I've ever read said that every border and sashing strip should be cut on the lengthwise grain. So I know how controversial it is when I say I prefer working with crossgrain strips. I love the little give in the crossgrain. That extra give makes it simpler to ease in the edges of a wobbly block. And I can cut strips from even a half-yard piece of fabric. The problem with crossgrain arises from twisting of the fabric as it is wound on the bolt. If we cut a crossgrain strip across fabric that has twisted, part of it will be straight, but a good portion of the strip will be practically on the bias. To cut true crossgrain strips, we must first line up the crossgrains; to do that, we have to tear across one end. If the cottons we usually use were woven as loosely as wool, we would pull a thread to straighten: the idea here is the same. After tearing the edge, we also have to cut off the frayed and distorted edge. Keep this in mind and add accordingly to yardage figures if your quilt shop cuts, not tears. (Shops will do one or the other, but not both.) Now we can line up the crossgrains and cut across the fabric: our pieces will be straight and in line with the grain. Because the crossgrain strips are limited to the width of the fabric, you may on occasion have to do some piecing. With a very small stitch (15 to the inch) and matching thread, you can make an almost invisible join.

Back to Setting...

Cut the strips the necessary width for your design plus ¼" seam allowance. From these long strips, cut as many short strips (look at your design and count) as you need. The short strips should measure the same as your block plus seam allowance at either end (example: 12" block = 12½" strip). Choose another fabric for the setting square, and cut it into squares the same width as the strip. If you look at your quilt diagram, you will see that there are two rows for this setting. The first row is: setting square to strip to square to strip to square. The second row is: strip to block to strip to block to strip. Alternate rows 1 and 2, finishing with row 1. If you press seams toward the strips in each row, the seams will lock together and matching is a breeze.

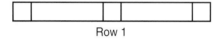
Row 1

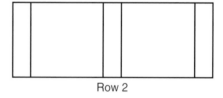
Row 2

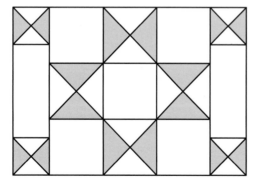

The basic method remains the same for fancier sets such as checkerboard, garden maze, or the creation of a new block at the setting square. Your diagram should give you all the answers you need. Let's look at the Ohio Star quilt as an example.

A new, smaller Ohio Star is created around the setting square. This means we must add pieced *Tricky* triangles to either end of the setting strip. The block is 9" square and the setting strip is 2" wide. Use 2" *Trickies* to piece the setting block, and sew them to either end of a 5½" x 2½" strip of setting fabric. The numbers add up, and the strip will measure 9" finished. Construct as many of these pieced strips as you need to finish your quilt. Sewing is the same as the simple set.

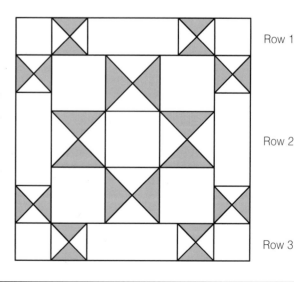
Row 1

Row 2

Row 3

The small Ohio Stars won't be complete without one more row of setting (you could think of it as the first border). In this case, we would cut 2½" x 9½" strips and alternate them with a pieced 2½" square of *Trickies*. This will finish up the small Ohio Stars.

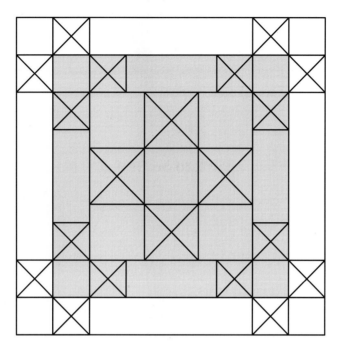

Whether you set your quilt together block-to-block or with any of the sashing options, the most important words I can leave you with are, "Make a diagram, and follow it." When the top is together, it is time to think about borders.

BORDERS

Not every quilt needs a border, but most quilts do look better with some kind of border. The border announces that the quilt is finished; it frames the piece and reiterates the fabrics and colors. The problem comes in deciding what to do for the border. I think about borders all the while I'm piecing the top. I make elaborate plans and reserve fabric, only to discover that my plan was crummy. The best time to choose borders is when the quilt top is sewn together. This is not very reassuring advice if your fabric supply is limited—but it's the reality. (If you think you have found the perfect fabric for the border, go ahead and buy it: it may become a part of your collection when you decide in favor of another fabric later.) The border should be harmonious with the quilt top, and subtle is better than overdone. (Incidentally, because I hate to waste fabric, I work on the border around one corner, usually the upper left.)

Let's look at some of our options. Because each quilt is different, I find it hard to make broad generalizations and will instead use some of my quilts as specific examples. I'll leave you free to draw your own conclusions as to what you like.

One way I like to think of borders is as a big picture frame with a multi-layered mat. The little rims of color around the quilt top re-introduce a color or colors from the body of the quilt and separate the background from the border. In that way I can use a "busy" background and a "busy" border and they won't mush together. Let's look at some examples in the small lily quilts (pages 34 and 35). In the peach and green piece I simply used a 1/2" rim of peach from the lilies and finished it off with the darkest of the greens. In the yellow and turquoise piece, the border is a repeat of the fabric I used as background in the center of the quilt. However, I think it would have been less effective without the little edge of red separating the border from the outside background. The red fabric appears nowhere in the quilt, but the color red is everywhere.

I'd like to dispel a myth of quiltmaking—that the border fabric must be in the body of the quilt: if you haven't used the fabric in the quilt, you can't use it in the border. I think that is baloney. Of course the two must relate. Neither of the border fabrics of the black floral lily appear in the middle. The first dark strip is rainbow ticking; it picked up all the colors of the flowers and contained the large floral background. I chose the next border because it looked as if the background had been sent through a grinder and came out in a finer-grained version. The border on the blue lily <u>makes</u> that quilt. I started with it, but then I realized it wouldn't be effective cut into small pieces. I chose all the center fabrics to look good with the large African print. The inner green and blue borders enhance the connection. Look at "Blessed Relief" (page 64), "Czech Hearts" (page 57), and the single heart hangings (page 57) as other examples of simple framing borders. Another little twist to the framing border can be seen in "Flower Dung Song" (page 33), "Barbed Wire" (page 123), "July" (page 60), "Good and Plenty" (page 63), and "Electric Slide" (page 64). Before adding any borders, I surrounded the top with a small strip of background fabric. This gives the design more room to breathe and keeps the colors at the edges from bleeding into the border. The border for "Electric Slide" (page 64) is a piano-key border of all the brilliant colors in the body of the quilt. That decision was made for two reasons: I couldn't decide on any one fabric as the perfect end of the quilt and, if I picked one fabric, I wouldn't have had enough to go around the quilt. The decision was practical as well as artistic. Because warm colors are more demanding of our attention, we need less of them, so they become the inner border. The blues, greens, and purples seemed like the perfect finish.

Look at "Peaky & Spike Go to Africa" (page 128) and "Flashback" (page 124). In both these quilts, I have slivered another color into the border. How do you know when this is the appropriate decision? I decided that when I could see that the fabric choice was perfect but too much of a good thing. The pink fabric around "Flashback" was almost eye-stabbing even as yardage, yet it was a perfect end to a very colorful quilt. To break that fabric up and calm it down (relatively speaking), I inserted varying widths of fabric from the center of the quilt. I think it made the border and the quilt.

The problem came up again with "Cheap Trick" (page 103). I would have loved just to slap that floral print on as a single border; but it was overwhelming on its own. The strip-pieced rainbow range with black outline broke up the floral border and related the blocks to the quilt.

Sometimes a design needs to be drawn out into the border to complete a pattern visually. This is most obvious in "Butter Churn" (page 103) and "Sally's Stars" (page 101). I needed to extend the light spikes into the border to complete what looked like four-pointed stars. If you put your finger over those points in the border, you'll see why they were necessary. Look at your own design for those clues. If you feel that you don't know how to end a pattern, maybe what you need is only part of the design extended into the border.

"Running Hot and Cold" (page 61) presented new problems for borders. Because one side of the quilt was hot colors and three sides were cool, no one fabric worked as a border for the whole quilt. I'm basically lazy and would have been thrilled to find a single border fabric, not to have worked so hard to finish this quilt. But the most logical finish was to use the darkest of the hot and cool fabrics to frame the center. Though the

Once you've made your decisions about the borders for a given quilt, you'll also want to face the fact that corners almost always look better when they are mitered. So, here is the method I find handiest, to avoid turning a simple process into the horror it's often rumored to be:

1. Press the strips to the quilt body; extend the strips to equal their width. (To make a beautiful miter with an intricately patterned strip, center a motif in the middle of each side.)
2. Sew the borders on from the wrong side of the quilt, and stitch to within ¼" of the end.
3. Fold the quilt top wrong sides together on the diagonal: the borders will line up.
4. Use a right-angle template, miter marker, or architect's right triangle to mark a line from the end of the stitching to the outside of the borders. Mark with a pencil and sew on the line; backstitch at the beginning and end.
5. Trim the excess border fabric to ¼" from the seam.

squares extend into the borders and the diagonal line of the reds continues, I still feel the quilt is finished because of the darkened edge.

All of this discussion of borders is my attempt to explain and perhaps justify decisions that made sense to me at the time I made the quilts. What I hope you get from all of this is that there are many options for borders. It is easy to poop out at this stage of the process and settle for the easiest, not necessarily the best, choice. Study the quilts in this book and in other books, antique and contemporary quilts at quilt shows and in magazines. Look at the borders to see how they have added or detracted from the overall image of the quilt. Are the borders so elaborate that they draw your eye away from the center? Or are they so simple they seem tacked on as a last resort? As you study what others have done, you will develop your own ideas. Keep an open mind and be willing to try more than one idea.

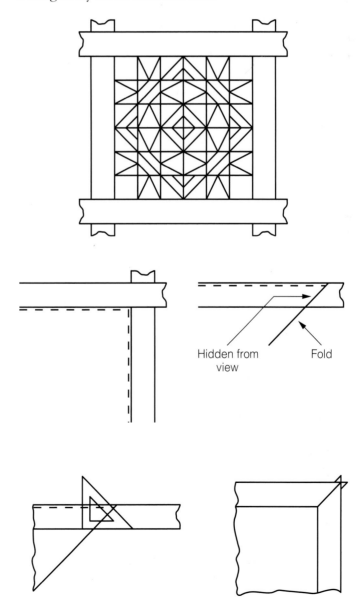

Hidden from view   Fold

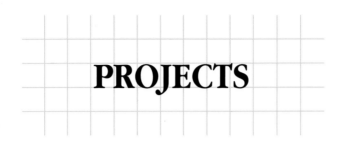

PROJECTS

I am including a small section of projects. This may sound contradictory, after all the energy I have spent persuading you to design your own quilts. However, by watching me lay out a project, you can follow my thought processes for a specific quilt and adapt those methods to your own piece. You may in fact want to start with one of my quilt designs, just to get used to the game. Though this procedure appears very organized, I want to go on record admitting that my personal working method is <u>slightly</u> more haphazard. For example, I never figured yardage for a complete quilt before I started cutting. But I have counted pieces and done a little figuring, if it appeared that I was going to run short of one of my fabric choices. If signs pointed to a drastic shortfall, I could start seeking a replacement fabric before all the pieces were cut out and the fabric used up. I find it very helpful and timesaving to scribble down a cutting plan—how many pieces of which fabric—before I start to cut the quilt. But, if you re-read the section on color, you'll see that I don't feel a fabric must stay in the quilt just because I've cut it up. More interesting ideas may come to you as your piece develops. For example, in the "African Lily," the idea of changing a section of the background came to me after everything was cut and laid out. Be open to this and let it happen.

Here are a few helpful hints before you start. Templates for all the projects are on the pull-out sheet in the back of the book. They are identified only by size. **All of these projects use 4" templates, so sort those out first.** Then, look at the units and templates that are laid out for your chosen project. Identify each piece by the appropriate letter. (If you look through all the projects, you'll notice that template A in one quilt is not necessarily template A in the next quilt.) For your projects, mark temporary letters on your templates (a neat chance to use the stick-on letters that come with VCR tapes!). Also note if the templates are reversing units (left- and right-handed) for the project; if so, you cut with the fabric doubled over. If your project calls for only one direction for the template, cut from a single layer of fabric.

On to the projects!

LILY PROJECTS

24" x 24" without borders, 34" x 34" finished (Pages 34 and 35)

These lily quilts grew from the original "Tidewater Lily" quilt, and from my urge to use *Mutt & Jeff* as reversing units. I love the spirit of the design and the color possibilities. Look at all the examples for inspiration, then have fun with your fabric stash. (Some of us have even seen corn in the lily design.)

Note that templates B and H are reversing units (right-handed and left-handed) and must be cut with fabric doubled to end up with the correct pieces. Template C is also a reverser but, in this particular quilt, you will need only the left-handed piece. Cut these pieces from a single layer. Note also that some templates appear in more than one unit—in this quilt, B and F.

St. Elsewhere
64" x 64"
hand quilted

Mini Gold Stars
23" x 23"
unquilted top

Topsy-Turvy
34" x 34"
hand quilted

Mini Barbed Wire
20" x 20"
unquilted top

Mini Peaky & Spike with Night & Noon
20" x 20"
unquilted top

Barbed Wire
77" x 62"
hand quilted

Peaky & Spike Go to the Great Barrier Reef
52" x 52"
hand quilted

Tidewater Lilies
80" x 63"
hand quilted

Flashback (Peaky & Spike
Go to Haight-Ashbury)
61" x 61"
hand quilted

Office Quilt
88" x 68"
hand quilted by the author and machine quilted by Cathy Ingram

Gulessarian Stars
65" x 50"
hand quilted

Sea of Stars
64" x 56"
hand quilted
Collection of Gisela and David Moyer

Peaky & Spike Go to Africa
(or Busch Gardens)
70" x 55"
hand quilted

Peaky & Spike with
Night & Noon
90" x 68"
hand quilted

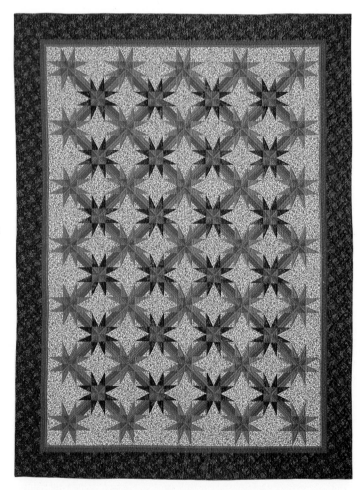

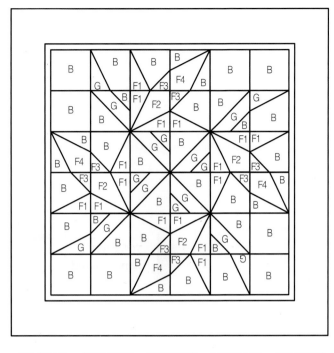

Units

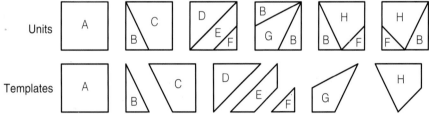

Templates

Cutting

FABRIC	TEMPLATE	NUMBER	YARDAGE
Background (B)	A	8	½ yard total
	B right & left	8	
	C	4	
	D	8	
	F	8	
	H right & left	8	
Leaf green (G)	E	8	¼ yard total
	B left	4	

Flower choices (I've used several related fabrics.)
Cut:

FABRIC	TEMPLATE	NUMBER	YARDAGE
Flower 1 (F1)	B	16	scraps
Flower 2 (F2)	G	4	
Flower 3 (F3)	F	8	
Flower 4 (F4)	G right & left	4	
Borders	4 strips	1½" x 27"	
	4 strips	4½" x 36"	
Backing	1¼ yards		

After all the pieces are cut, lay them out on your design surface. The best time to make changes is before you sew. Look at the entire quilt now, to be sure you are happy with your choices.

Sewing

Sew individual units together. Refer to the section on machine sewing for details. When units are sewn and pressed, and overhanging points are trimmed off, you can begin assembling the quilt. Put together these nine sections.

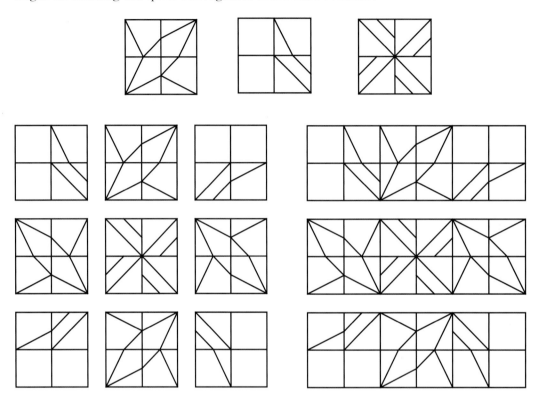

AMBROSIA

96" x 75" (Page 99)

Ambrosia is a queen-size quilt constructed of 12 five-patch blocks. Made with 4" units, each block measures 20" square. They are put together with 1" setting strips, followed by a ½" border and then a 5" border. I used warm colors in the crossbars of this five-patch block and cool fabrics in the corner sections. Though I have made quilts that are visually more complicated, I love the freshness and simplicity of both color and design in "Ambrosia." If you use 3" units instead of 4", the finished piece will measure 76" x 60".

Fabric

Background:	Cream (C)	2¼ yards (total for all)
Corners	Blue #1 (B1)	¾ yard
	Blue #2 (B2)	½ yard
	Green #1 (G1)	¾ yard
	Green #2 (G2)	1 yard
	Cream (C)	(see above)
Crossbars	Red Purple (Rp)	½ yard
	Pink (Pk)	¾ yard
	Peachy Pink (Pp)	½ yard
	Peach (P)	½ yard
	Light Peach (Lp)	½ yard
	Cream (C)	(see above)
Center	Purple (Pr)	¼ yard
	Yellow (Y)	¼ yard

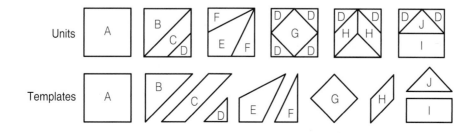

Cutting

	Template	No. in Block	x	Blocks in Quilt	=	Total
Cream	A	4	x	12	=	48
	B	8	x	12	=	96
	D	8	x	12	=	96
Blue #1	E	4	x	12	=	48
Blue #2	D	8	x	2	=	96
Green #1	F (l & r)	8	x	12	=	96
Green #2	C	8	x	12	=	96
Purple	G	1	x	12	=	12
Yellow	D	4	x	12	=	48
Red Purple	J	4	x	12	=	48
Pink	H (l & r)	8	x	12	=	96
Peachy Pink	D	8	x	12	=	96
Peach	I	4	x	12	=	48
Light Peach	J	4	x	12	=	48

Setting strip — Sky Blue: Cut 31 strips 1½" x 20½". (3/4 yard)

Setting Square — Dark Sky Blue: Cut 20 squares 1½". (leftover fabric from final border)

First narrow border — I used a narrow purple stripe cut crossgrain. Cut eight 1" strips and sew them together to create the lengths. (¼ yard)

Final border — Dark Sky Blue: 3 yards: Cut 2 strips 5½" x 108". Cut lengthwise 2 strips 5½" x 80".

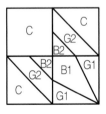 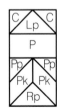

Lay out the cut fabric for one block. The colors for crossbars should flow from dark to light, red purple through pink to peach. Greens and blues should be in the medium range, with the C's darkest of the four fabrics. Sew the units together and trim off the mouse ears. Sew the four corner units, the crossbars, and center square together. Then sew the three rows together.

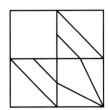 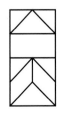 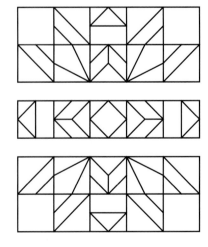

To assemble the quilt, sew setting square to strip to square to strip to square to strip to square. Then sew strip to block to strip to block across the row. Sew skinny row to row of blocks, until the whole quilt is together. Then add borders.

PEAKY & SPIKE AND FRIENDS

56" x 48" before borders (Page 40)

This quilt is great fun to make and a great way to sample many of the components that this book is based on. It is a variation of the rectangular Card Trick but, instead of following the central core with row upon row of Card Trick units, I used *Flying Geese, Wingy Things, Half Night & Noons, Center Diamonds, Ice Cream Cones II,* and *Peaky & Spikes.* Though yardage and instructions are given for a wallhanging or a lap-size quilt, it would be relatively easy to make this bed-size by adding borders between the rows of the units. Feel free as well to substitute units, such as *Four-Patches* for *Center Diamonds.* The fabrics are arranged in rainbow order: red, orange, yellow, green, blue, violet, on a consistent background. I think this would be a great design to do in scrap as well. Another possibly interesting twist would be changing the background of each round: darker toward the center, lighter toward the edge.

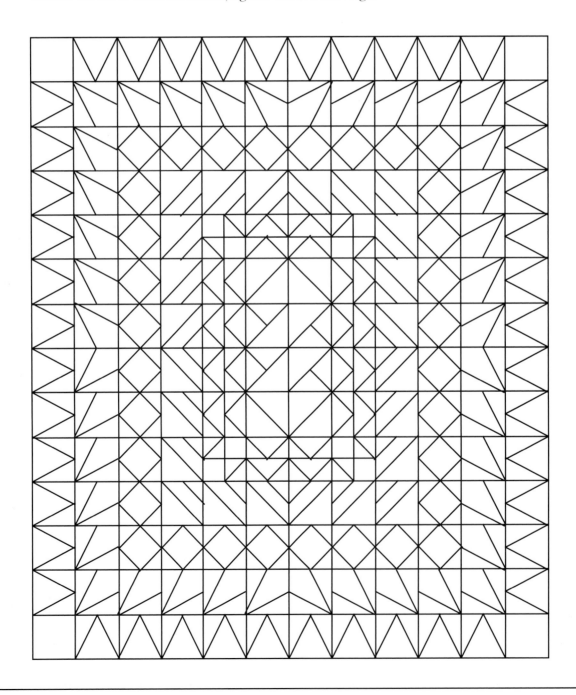

Fabric

Total Background (M)		1¾ yards w/o border
		2¼ yards w/border
Round 1	Red #1 (R1)	scrap 5" x 20"
	Red #2 (R2)	scrap 3" x 16"
Round 2	Orange #1 (O1)	¼ yard
	Orange #2 (O2)	¼ yard
Round 3	Yellow #1 (Y1)	½ yard
	Yellow #2 (Y2)	¼ yard
Round 4	Green #1 (G1)	½ yard
	Green #2 (G2)	¼ yard
Round 5	Blue #1 (B1)	½ yard
	Blue #2 (B2)	¼ yard
Round 6	Purple #1 (P1)	¼ yard
	Purple #2 (P2)	¼ yard

Units

Templates

To cut all background, here are the totals:

4" right triangle A	4 + 24	=	28
4" triangle B	4	=	4
2" right triangle C	32 + 68	=	100
2" square D	4	=	4
2x4 Peaky G	44	=	44
4" Spike I	44	=	44
4" square J	4	=	4

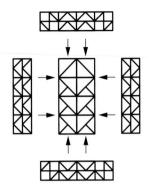

Sew all units together; clip off the mouse ears and lay out the units on your design surface. To assemble the quilt, work from the center to the outside.

Sew the units into rows and attach them to the center on both sides. Sew the top and bottom rows and attach them to what you have previously sewn. Do the same for each round.

I added a final border of 2" in background fabric and called it quits.

Another border at this point might look great if you can co-ordinate it to the body of the quilt.

You would need to purchase at least 1½ yards to cut borders on the lengthwise grain.

Cutting

		TEMPLATE	TOTAL
Center	R1	A	8
Round 1	R2	B	4
	M	A	4
	M	B	4
Round 2	O1	B	32
	O1	C	8
	O2	C	24
	O2	D	4
	M	C	32
	M	D	4
Round 3	Y1	E	24
	Y2	C	24
	M	A	24
Round 4	G1	F	32
	G2	C	60
	M	C	68
Round 5	B1	H	40
	B2	G (r & l)	36
	M	G (r & l)	44
Round 6	P1	G (r & l)	48
	P2	G(r & l)	40
	M	I	44
	M	J	4

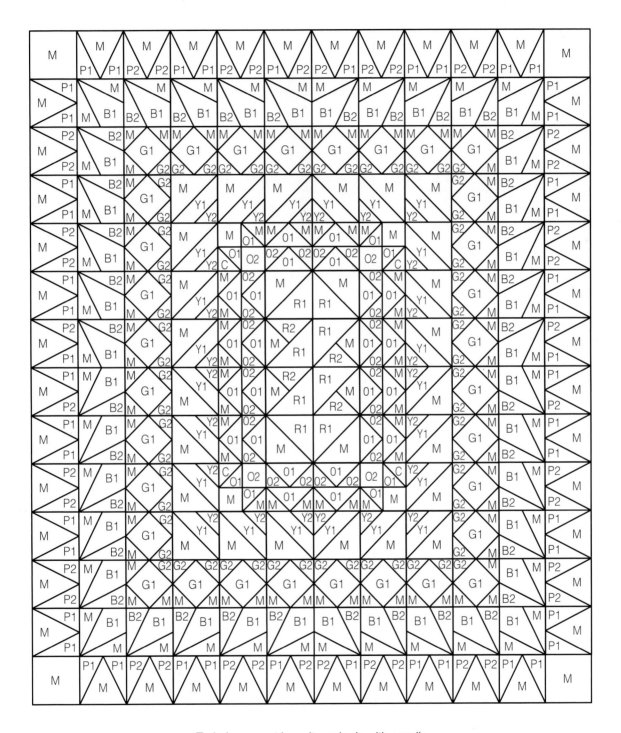

To help prevent insanity, color in with pencils.

This is the same design, with the center expanded and 2" strips between the rounds.
Of course, you will need additional fabric.

CHRISTMAS ROSE

48" x 48" (Page 102)

The design is created from simple, easy-to-sew alternating blocks but, with clever fabric placement, a medallion of sorts appears. Constructed with 4" units, the top will measure 36" square before borders, 48" with borders.

Fabric

Red #1	(R1)	½ yard + 6" if used in border
Red #2	(R2)	¼ yard
Green #1	(G1)	¼ yard
Green #2	(G2)	¼ yard + 25" for border (total 1 yard)
Multi red/green	(M)	½ yard
Cream	(C)	½ yard

Cutting instructions are for the whole quilt top. For example, template E is used in both center and corner blocks. You will cut 4 of color G1 for the center block and 16 for the four corner blocks, for a total of 20 E's of fabric G1.

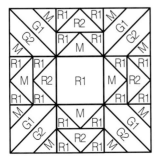
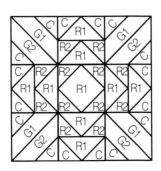
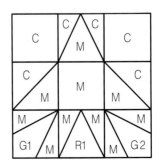

Units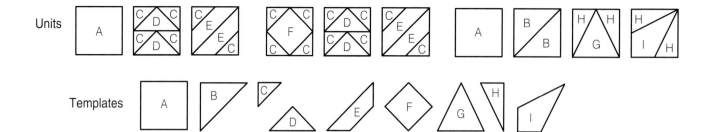

Templates

Cutting

Template	No. in block	x	blocks in quilt	=	Total
Red #1 (R1) (darker)					
A	1	x	1	=	1
C	16	x	1	=	16
D	8	x	4	=	32
F	1	x	4	=	4
G	1	x	4	=	4
Red #2 (R2) (lighter)					
C	12	x	4	=	48
D	4	x	1	=	4
Green #1 (G1) (lighter)					
E	4 x 1 = 4	+	4 x 4 = 16	=	20
I	1	x	4	=	4
Green #2 (G2) (darker)					
E	4 x 1 = 4	+	4 x 4 = 16	=	20
I	1	x	4	=	4
Multi red/green (M)					
C	8	x	1	=	8
D	4	x	1	=	4
A	1	x	4	=	4
B	2	x	4	=	8
G	1	x	4	=	4
H	6	x	4	=	24
Cream (C)					
A	2	x	4	=	8
B	2	x	4	=	8
C	16	x	4	=	64
H	2	x	4	=	8

When all the pieces have been cut, lay them on a design surface. Make sure you like what you see, then sew. Instructions for sewing are in Chapter 4.

Assemble the units into nine-patch blocks, then join the blocks in rows and sew the rows together.

Add the borders. The first border on my quilt is a narrow strip of Red #1, followed by the Multi red/green, also fairly narrow. The last border should be at least 4" finished.

"Gulessarian Stars"

"Flower Dung Song"

"Tidewater Lilies"

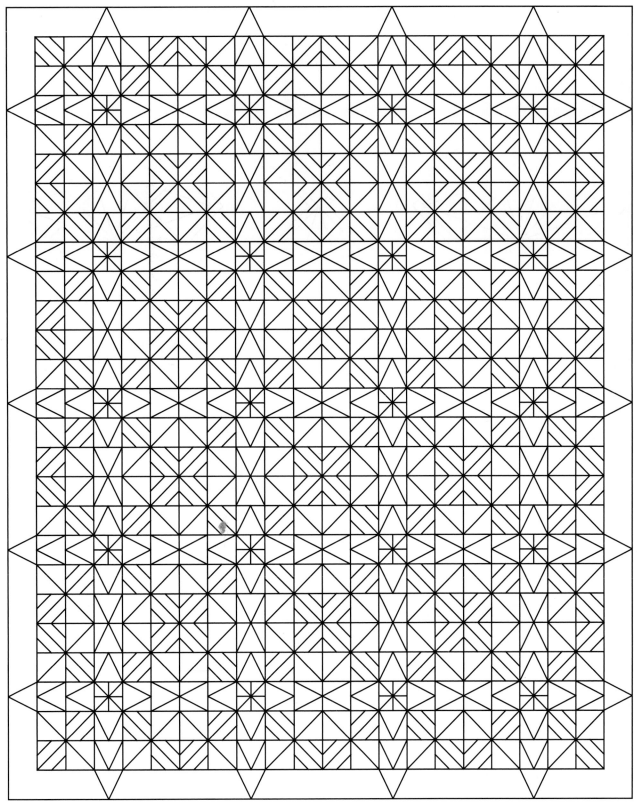

"Harold's Quilt"

"St. Elsewhere"

"Barbed Wire"

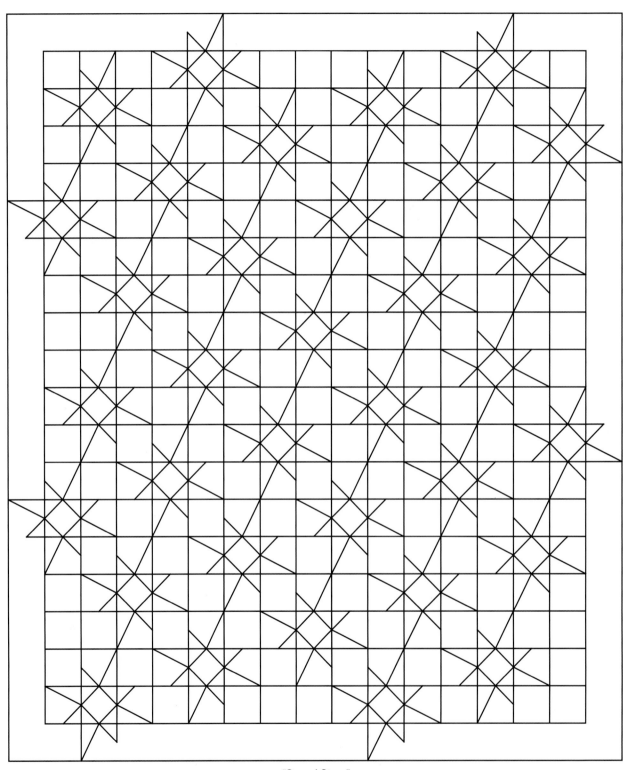

"Sea of Stars"

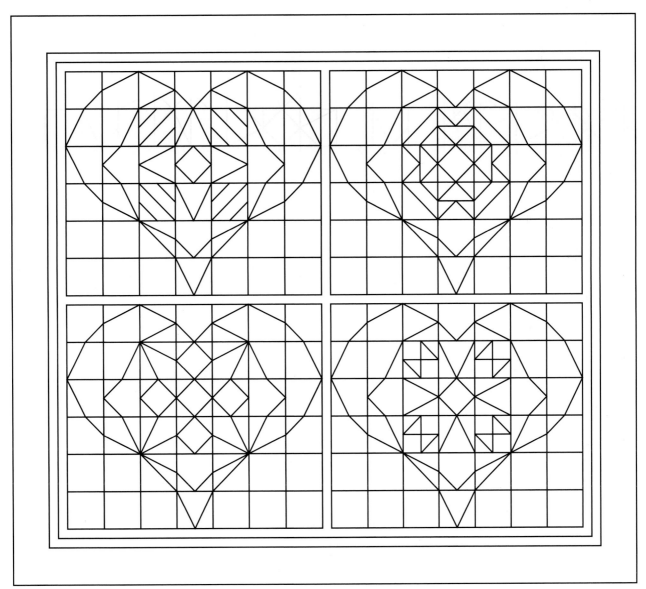

"Pink Hearts"

"Bahamian Blossoms"

"Cross Street Pasture"

"Cheap Trick"

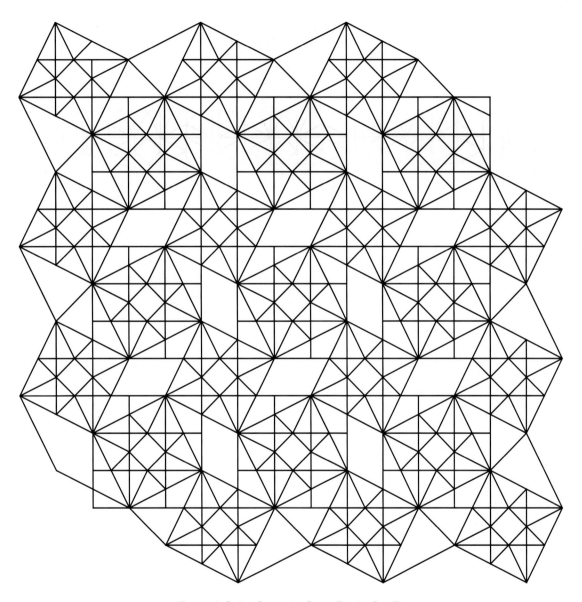

"Peaky & Spike Go to the Great Barrier Reef"

154

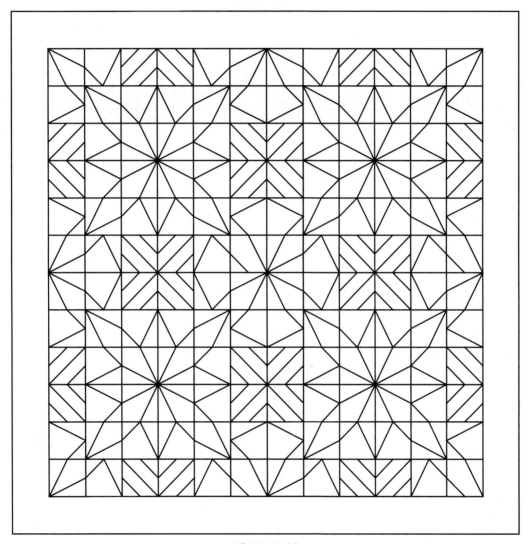

"Prickly Itch"

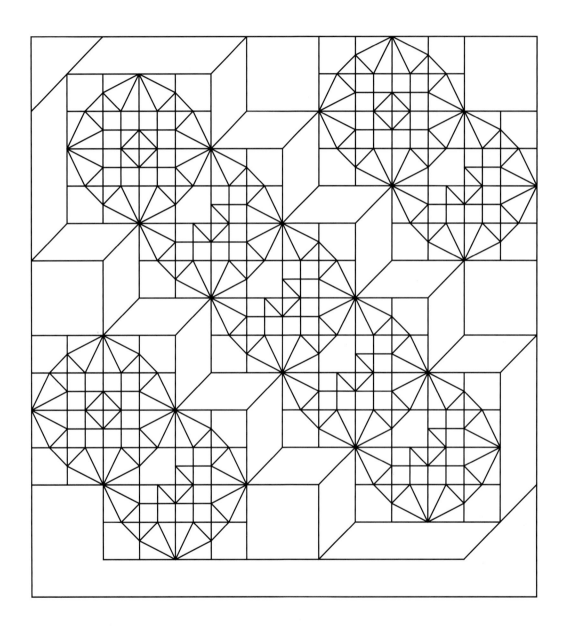

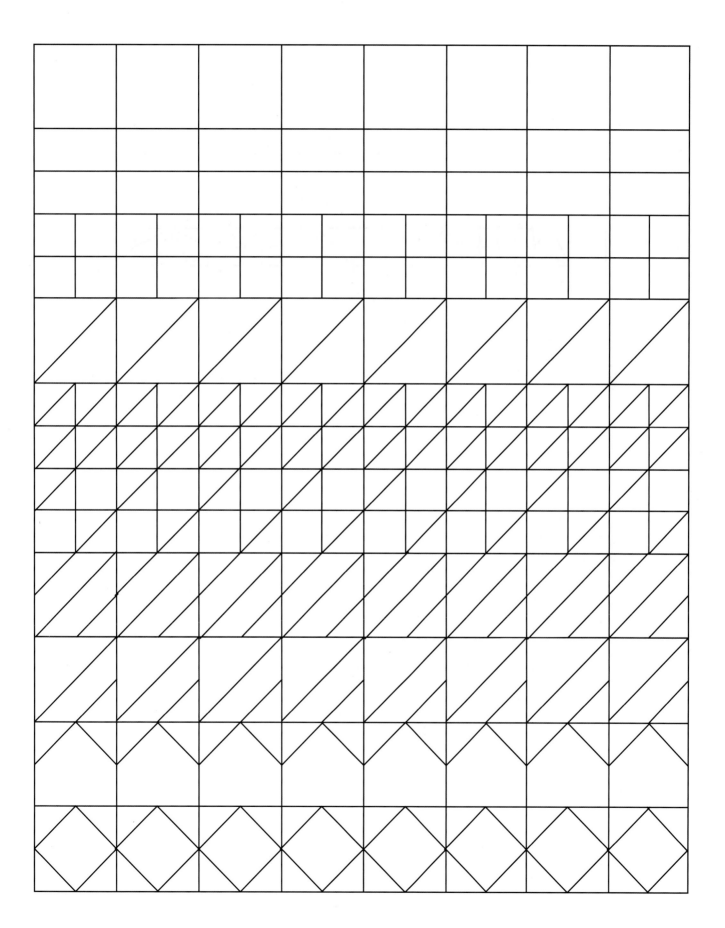

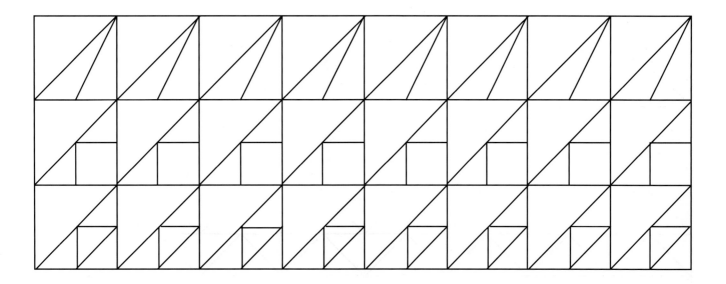

Other Fine Quilting Books from C & T Publishing

An Amish Adventure, Roberta Horton
Appliqué 12 Easy Ways!, Elly Sienkiewicz
The Art of Silk Ribbon Embroidery, Judith Montano
Baltimore Album Quilts, Historic Notes and Antique Patterns, Elly Sienkiewicz
Baltimore Beauties and Beyond (2 Volumes), Elly Sienkiewicz
The Best From Gooseberry Hill, Patterns for Stuffed Animals and Dolls, Kathy Pace
A Celebration of Hearts, Jean Wells and Marina Anderson
Christmas Traditions From the Heart, Margaret Peters
Crazy Quilt Handbook, Judith Montano
Crazy Quilt Odyssey, Judith Montano
Design a Baltimore Album Quilt!, Elly Sienkiewicz
Dimensional Appliqué—Baskets, Blooms & Borders, Elly Sienkiewicz
Friendship's Offering, Susan McKelvey
Heirloom Machine Quilting, Harriet Hargrave
Imagery on Fabric, Jean Ray Laury
Isometric Perspective, Katie Pasquini-Masopust
Landscapes & Illusions, Joen Wolfrom
The Magical Effects of Color, Joen Wolfrom
Mastering Machine Appliqué, Harriet Hargrave
Memorabilia Quilting, Jean Wells
NSA Series: Bloomin' Creation, Jean Wells
NSA Series: Holiday Magic, Jean Wells
NSA Series: Hometown, Jean Wells
NSA Series: Hearts, Fans, Folk Art, Jean Wells
PQME Series: Milky Way Quilt, Jean Wells
PQME Series: Nine-Patch Quilt, Jean Wells
PQME Series: Pinwheel Quilt, Jean Wells
PQME Series: Stars & Hearts Quilt, Jean Wells
Quilts, Quilts, and More Quilts!, Diana McClun and Laura Nownes
Recollections, Judith Montano
Stitching Free: Easy Machine Pictures, Shirley Nilsson
Story Quilts, Mary Mashuta
Three-Dimensional Design, Katie Pasquini
A Treasury of Quilt Labels, Susan McKelvey
Visions: The Art of the Quilt, Quilt San Diego
Whimsical Animals, Miriam Gourley

For more information write for a free catalog from
C & T Publishing
P.O. Box 1456
Lafayette, CA 94549
(1-800-284-1114)